"Lately I've encountered lots of sp[...] most of those emotionally overw[...] whiney and wiser-than-thou. This one is refreshingly different. It's built around an actual story, with a beginning, middle and end. It's a great story too, told by a likable, honest, regular guy who just happens to really know how to write. By the time you finish it, Kent Annan will be your friend; he'll have learned a lot, and so will you."

Bart Campolo, urban minister

"It's not often you read a book at once as moving and disturbing as Kent Annan's accounts of the time he has lived among the rural poor of Haiti, where every day tested his fortitude, his marriage and his abundant store of good humor. Yet he doesn't wish to play on our feelings or to point an accusing finger. Rather, he wants to share his fears, his bewilderment, and the everyday glimmers of beauty and joy he finds among his neighbors."

Aina Barten, features editor, *Orion Magazine*

"An unpredictable book! As you read this story, words like *fascinating, convicting* and *inspiring* will come to mind, but beneath them you will feel the suffering strain—and yes, the glory—of a young couple radically following Jesus into the lives of the obscenely poor people of Haiti."

Tony Campolo, founder, Evangelical Association for the Advancement of Education

"Kent Annan is a gifted writer to keep an eye on with a message you can't afford to miss. Highly recommended!"

Margaret Feinberg, author, *Scouting the Divine* and *The Organic God*

"*Following Jesus Through the Eye of the Needle* is a fresh and accessible memoir of hope and discovery. Kent Annan's journey is an invitation for all of us to consider how we might find authentic ways to love faithfully and live humbly. In a world that desperately needs a good God to be embodied, Kent Annan offers himself as an answer to that prayer."

Christopher L. Heuertz, author, *Simple Spirituality,* and international director, Word Made Flesh

Following Jesus
Through the Eye of the Needle

LIVING FULLY, LOVING DANGEROUSLY

KENT ANNAN

IVP Books

An imprint of InterVarsity Press
Downers Grove, Illinois

InterVarsity Press
P.O. Box 1400, Downers Grove, IL 60515-1426
World Wide Web: www.ivpress.com
E-mail: email@ivpress.com

InterVarsity Press® is the book-publishing division of InterVarsity Christian Fellowship/USA®, a movement of students and faculty active on campus at hundreds of universities, colleges and schools of nursing in the United States of America, and a member movement of the International Fellowship of Evangelical Students. For information about local and regional activities, write Public Relations Dept., InterVarsity Christian Fellowship/USA, 6400 Schroeder Rd., P.O. Box 7895, Madison, WI 53707-7895, or visit the IVCF website at <www.intervarsity.org>.

All Scripture quotations, unless otherwise indicated, are taken from the Holy Bible, New International Verison®. NIV®. Copyright ©1973, 1978, 1984 by International Bible Society. Used by permission of Zondervan Publishing House. All right reserved.

The author is very grateful to the following journals and magazines for publishing parts of this book: Subtropics, The Sun, Natural Bridge, Pilgrimage, Orion, The Other Side, Geez, Adbusters, Puerto Del Sol and Utne Reader.

The author is grateful for permission to quote from "A Brief for the Defense" from Refusing Heaven: Poems by Jack Gilbert, copyright ©2005 by Jack Gilbert. Used by permission of Alfred A. Knopf, a division of Random House, Inc.

While all the stories in this book are based on real people and events, some names, identifying details and locations have been altered to protect the privacy of the individuals involved.

Design: Cindy Kiple

Images: front cover: Port au Prince, Haiti. Angela Catlin/Corbis
Back cover images provided by the author and used by permission.

ISBN 978-0-8308-3730-4

Printed in the United States of America ∞

 InterVarsity Press is committed to protecting the environment and to the responsible use of natural resources. As a member of Green Press Initiative we use recycled paper whenever possible. To learn more about the Green Press Initiative, visit <www.greenpressinitiative.org>.

Library of Congress Cataloging-in-Publication Data

Annan, Kent, 1973-
Following Jesus through the eye of the needle: living fully, loving dangerously / Kent Annan.
    p. cm.
ISBN 978-0-8308-3730-4 (pbk.: alk. paper)
1. Annan, Kent, 1973- 2. Missionaries—Haiti—Biography. 3.
Missionaries—United States—Biography. 4. Haiti—Social
conditions—1971- I. Title.
BV2848.H4A553 2009
266'.0237307294092—dc22
[B B]
                                                            2009031639

P   18   17   16   15   14   13   12   11   10   9   8   7   6   5   4   3   2   1
Y   24   23   22   21   20   19   18   17   16   15   14   13   12   11   10   09

For and with Shelly

Contents

5. Revelations

6. Next Steps

As Jesus started on his way, a man ran up to him and
fell on his knees before him. "Good Teacher," he asked,
"what must I do to inherit eternal life?"

"Why do you call me good?" Jesus answered.
"No one is good—except God alone.
You know the commandments: 'Do not murder, do not commit adultery,
do shall not steal, do not give false testimony, do not defraud,
honor your father and mother.'"

"Teacher," he declared, "all these I have kept since I was a boy."

Jesus looked at him and loved him. "One thing you lack," he said.
"Go, sell everything you have and give to the poor, and you
will have treasure in heaven. Then come, follow me."

At this the man's face fell. He went away sad,
because he had great wealth.

Jesus looked around and said to his disciples,
"How hard it is for the rich to enter the kingdom of God!"

The disciples were amazed at his words. But Jesus said
again, "Children, how hard it is to enter the kingdom of God!
It is easier for a camel to go through the eye of a needle than for
a rich man to enter the kingdom of God."

The disciples were even more amazed, and said to each other,
"Who then can be saved?"

Jesus looked at them and said, "With man this is impossible,
but not with God; all things are possible with God."

MARK 10:17-27

---1---

Through the Needle's Eye

REASONS TO FOLLOW (AND MAKE A DIFFERENCE)

The blue-collar, callous-handed guys roll their eyes as the well-dressed young man walks up. It doesn't help that his opening line to Jesus is, "What must I do to earn eternal life?"

"Of course," whispers Peter to Thomas, "who wouldn't want to keep living forever if your bank account will last that long?"

Jesus ignores his disciples. "All you have to do," he tells the eager young man, "is everything God considers good—all those rules Moses came down the mountain with."

"I'm faithful to all that," says the young man.

Jesus shoots Peter and Thomas a look. They stay quiet. It would be easy to mock this rich guy's self-righteousness, but they're also disconcerted as they recognize in him the same awkward mix of eagerness and desperation that started them trekking around behind a holy, baffling Messiah.

Then Jesus steps closer to the young man, leans in, puts his hand gently on the back of his head and whispers into his ear.

Jesus pulls back slowly. The young man looks up to find his eyes. Then his shoulders slump, wind knocked out of him. What did Jesus say? He looks again at Jesus, who stands quietly. The young man turns. He walks away.

I've walked away too. I've spent long stretches living with those same slumped shoulders. Other times I've tried to pull back my shoulders and do what it takes to follow. Neither is easy. Grace is needed. This story is about the stumbles and joys of trying to follow—trying to make a difference for other people and for my own life—instead of turning away.

The TV news shows and online news streams work to keep us riveted to tragedy after tragedy. Each upcoming story is crucial. Then fifteen or thirty minutes later, there's nothing you can do about all you've seen, which spans the country and the globe, except feel punished and depleted in mind and soul. And there are the charity ads, the local fundraisers, the church announcements. There are ways to volunteer that feel meaningful, but how can it not seem too little? Focus on the demands of your family, friends and work, as if that weren't more than enough.

But it nags, doesn't it? Gets caught a little in the throat. Should I, could I, be doing something that really makes a difference? What would it look like? What do I really believe about helping other people, especially if it gets demanding?

And, really, can I just decide that I have to—that I *get to*—try?

For me, after college a mix of adventure, faith and idealism compelled me to work with a refugee ministry in Europe. I became friends with guys my age who had fled as refugees from ugly wars in Sarajevo or Sierra Leone. I sat with families torn apart by suffering and poverty that before I'd known only as headlines or political science topics. It was good and uncomfortable connecting to the world in a personal way.

I returned to the United States to study more. I married my beautiful wife. Happier than I'd ever been in many ways, I still felt like I'd walked away. My shoulders started slumping again. (This is where I should quote Mother Teresa on how our love for God and our love for neighbors in need is intertwined, but let's skip that formality.) There's a world out there with two billion people living on less than two dollars a day. Too many people can't find enough calories. Too many children live in virtual slavery.

And they aren't just statistics. I've played marbles with children who have never been able to spend a single day in school. I've talked with the dads out in the stingy farm fields. I've sat next to the moms cooking rice—the one meager meal for the day—over a pile of twigs.

So I moved to Haiti with my long-suffering wife (more on that later). We went with Beyond Borders, a small grass-roots organization that seemed to approach things differently. While this organization works on education issues, they take so seriously the idea of not turning away that they offer few comforts to their American staff. We moved in with a Haitian peasant family twenty-four hours after we arrived in the country—with an overnight orientation, and then only occasional visits to ensure we were okay. They required us to move into this new community with only one backpack of belongings and no money except living expenses to give to the family we stayed with.

Our job for the first seven months was to start learning the language and culture—not from books or classes, but from the people around us. In a village meeting before we arrived, people were asked what they would be willing to teach us. At first they resisted—unsure about foreigners coming and also wondering what they could teach educated (and presumably rich) foreigners. But as the conversation progressed, they began to understand that we were coming as learners who were basically helpless and in their hands. People started volunteering: "I'll take them out to the fields." "I'll show them how to cook rice over the fire."

Now I've been working on education issues in Haiti for seven years—sometimes living there and sometimes traveling back and forth from the United States. This story is about the personal experience (more so than the work) of living in Haiti, where I began disoriented in that village.

What does Jesus whisper that I must give up so I can become more alive? What's it like to love—and be loved by—other people in circumstances far different from our own? What are the benefits of trying, as much as it's possible, to face suffering and find ways to alleviate it?

Of course I don't have all the answers. This is an adventure in stumbling and sometimes finding. After the rich young man slumped off, Jesus said it's harder for a rich man to enter the kingdom of heaven than it is for a camel to squeeze through the eye of a needle. If you've picked up this book, you're likely rich by a lot of standards: even access to books and the education to be literate can't be taken for granted. So you and I, Jesus whispers in our ears—and it seems worth trying to squeeze through the needle's eye so we can help and learn more about love.

Guilt, compassion, grace and trusting that Jesus invites us toward what is good—these all motivate me. It's not easy, and I've failed a lot. But I've also found something about freedom and joy that I never found in other ways—even though on the other side of the needle I also occasionally find a sawed-off shotgun aiming haphazardly at my knees . . .

Work out your salvation with fear and trembling.

PHILIPPIANS 2:12

Abraham fell facedown; he laughed.

GENESIS 17:17

OUTSIDE THE GATES

Jonas has a friendly, almost naive smile. I cringe sometimes walking by the sawed-off shotgun sitting across his lap—aimed too casually at my knees. From Internet cafés like this one to small grocery stores with less wares than a U.S. 7-Eleven, all kinds of Haitian businesses have guards stationed at their entrances these days.

I take a seat at one of the computers. My wife, Shelly, sits two cubicles down.

"Yours working?"

"Barely. Yours?"

Three of the seven computers work today. Not bad. The e-mail home page creeps onto the screen like a glacier, though it's sweaty in the Internet café and out on the Port-au-Prince streets.

We come here for an hour several times a week to work and stay in touch with friends and family. Jonas, the security guard, sits on his plastic chair just inside the door of this small room of computers and phones. The windows look out from the second floor onto a busy street. Tangles of electrical wires are suspended on poles overhead as people sell, walk, buy, push wheelbarrows, honk horns, laugh and shout under the unblinking sun.

Voices are getting louder outside. A demonstration might be coming near. We're just down the street from Place St. Pierre, a large public square where some of these have started as the political situation continues to heat up.

I look up from the computer screen and see the women who run the café looking nervous. One walks over to lock the back door. Jonas holds his gun as he stands to look out the front.

Recently I talked with a different guard at someone's office. I asked him how much he made—about sixty dollars a month to try to support himself and his family. That doesn't inspire confidence—and I hope he doesn't sacrifice himself for that salary if something actually does happen.

The chants are getting closer. I call Shelly over to watch out the window as the march approaches. There has been some violence, but not in this part of the city. Being on the street as the crowd goes by doesn't seem smart, but I don't think there's any danger. Then thousands of chanting people round the corner with incredible energy.

Jonas locks the door. There's nothing for us to do but keep trying to work. The Internet connection is moving too slowly for Shelly and me to send flirting e-mails like we do sometimes. And what would I type?

"Hi, cutie. Ain't danger exciting?—Your loving, protecting husband."

She might not find that funny at the moment.

Then, *boom*. What was that? A gunshot. There's a frantic scene outside the door. Jonas is out there. He's banging on the door. The women unlock it. People are yelling. Jonas squeezes in, and they lock the door again. He's nervous. "They were crowding in on the balcony. I just shot in the air."

Okay, this isn't going well. We're trapped. I pray Jonas didn't shoot anyone. I pray that he'll put that gun down. Do I crawl under the cubicle with Shelly? Okay, I'm a little scared. This is stupid. I'm not outside marching, and it doesn't seem like my business. I'm just trying to send two-sentence e-mails about our work and the country. What do I possibly have to contribute to "development" in a situation like this? I'm busy wondering if I should take my wife and go hide in the bathroom and hope the crowd passes by and Jonas settles down. So this is how I'm trying to change the world and save my soul?

⌒

Half an hour later we walk through the normal bustle toward the pickup that, for seven gouds (twenty cents), gives us a ride in the truck's bed up toward our house. My eyes scan for signs of danger—just like a Hollywood action hero, except that all I could do if I find danger is grab my wife's hand and run.

The trip home is fine, but the national situation keeps getting worse as a mixture of truth, lies and rumors swirls at increasing velocity: A body lies in the middle of a dirt road near where we live, tennis shoes poking out from under the cardboard and branches laid over it, flies buzzing around. Political demonstrations spin out of control as pro-government gangs swoop in with clubs and guns. Plumes of smoke rise from burning tires at intersections around the city. Roadblocks manned by angry young men pop up at random—they might take your car, or much more. A man in a wheelchair whom we saw regularly in the city on the way to work is murdered for his political views. Eleven radio stations are ransacked. Three foreign journalists are hacked to death by an angry mob. Whispers circulate that those in power are offering human sacrifices, including pregnant women, to spiritual powers. A French woman is kidnapped. The rebels are coming. Helicopters—an overhead *whir* that usually means the president is on the move—are busier each night. President Jean-Bertrand Aristide announces he will fight to the death. The CIA is the engine driving the rebellion. U.S. Marines come in to protect the American Embassy, and ships are stationed offshore to ensure Haitians don't escape to safety on South Florida's beaches. We receive phone calls and e-mails from incredulous friends and family asking, "Why haven't you left yet?" The "rebels" are coming closer to Port-au-Prince—and with them the potential for a chaotic civil war between insurgents and gangs, both heavily armed. Police strip off their uniforms and dash for the hills. Jails around the country empty.

Shelly and I face the decision of whether or not to leave. We've been working in Haiti just over a year. We talk with many Haitian and American friends and coworkers. All of them say it would probably be safe for us to stay, but wise to go. To one Haitian colleague in our office I say, "It's awful. I can just get on a flight and leave, but you can't." The fact hangs there a moment. Then he shakes his head and says, "I know, but I'm taking my wife and two kids to stay with family in the countryside. Go. Go and come back, and we'll be together after things settle down." We hug and return to figuring out our respective plans.

The "rebels" have just taken over the north of the country without much resistance, and a clash in Port-au-Prince, the president's power base, seems imminent. The U.S. State Department issues a warning: "This travel warning is being issued to inform American citizens that, due to the continued unrest and a steady deterioration of the security situation in Haiti, including violent confrontations between pro- and anti-government forces . . . the Department of State strongly urges American citizens to depart the country . . . at their first safe opportunity."

Haitian radio stations and our neighbors are daily spinning out worst-case scenarios of societal breakdown. President Aristide predicts a "blood bath." Shelly and I talk every day about what to do and how to decide. I find myself awake at 3 a.m. weighing fears against ideals—not as an abstract exercise, but to decide whether to call American Airlines in the morning.

I imagine living with each decision: staying or going. I know going would carry some regrets, whereas staying would result either in no regrets or devastating consequences. We consider the possibility of Shelly going and me staying. Chances are that I would be safe if I kept out of the city. But maybe there is also the chance of a messy, prolonged civil war. Would people target me, a foreigner, on the presumption that I had money or things worth stealing? I couldn't do my job if it wasn't safe to move around. I could accomplish more from Florida. Or maybe this is all exaggeration.

Sleep is fitful, dreams troubled. I question my own integrity. Pride (it's pitiful but true) urges me to stay: I would secretly enjoy being able to say that I had lived through a coup, which would somehow boost my legitimacy. Fear and the survival instinct—as well as the love that compels me to protect and be with Shelly—tells me to go. But I don't want to abandon the people I came here to live with and work alongside. But there isn't anything I can do in this situation. And so it goes, round and round.

~

The Christian home and culture I grew up in held in highest esteem missionaries and others who sacrificed on behalf of the unevangelized or poor in distant lands. Photos of missionaries were displayed on church walls, and most homes had missionary prayer cards on their refrigerators. *Through Gates of Splendor*, the account of five young missionaries who died in their attempt to spread the gospel in Ecuador in 1956, was popular reading. Throughout my childhood, heroes of the faith would occasionally sit at our dining-room table, and I would listen quietly, enthralled by tales of their noble adventures.

Through my experience, I'd come to dismiss the aspect of this faith culture that put these people on too high a pedestal. Yet I did sign up for related work. I had explored other possibilities in college, but nothing seemed as meaningful or interesting to me as serving people who most needed help, especially people in far-off places. After college a family friend (who had appeared occasionally at our family dinner table) convinced me to work with a refugee ministry in Western Europe, which eventually led me to Albania and Kosovo and now to Haiti, where I was choosing whether to stay or leave.

In trying to decide, I feel unable to find the balance between sacrifice and caution, love and prudence, safety and risk. My natural (selfish) inclination is to maximize my contributions to goodness while minimizing personal risk. (Which isn't to say I'm never rash: just to avoid a couple of miserable, sweaty hours of Port-au-Prince traffic, I often ride motorcycle taxis without a helmet along streets where I've seen lifeless bodies laid out next to crumpled bikes.) My hope that life goes on after death and divine grace awaits should strengthen me to hold my life more loosely and give more recklessly, but I'm enough of a doubter that the possibility of death is still plenty daunting.

Becoming increasingly protective of my life comes from growing older and cherishing gifts like marriage, work, family, friendships. But this is potentially corrosive if it eats away at boldness in love. The world is in bad enough shape that it takes strong, risky action to make a difference, doesn't it?

A decision is needed. Airports are expected to close any day. The situation in the city is rapidly deteriorating into violent chaos. With the lights of Port-au-Prince down below, I sit on our porch vacillating. I want to protect myself and Shelly, but also to be vulnerable to love's persuasive power.

～

Choices both reveal and make us. There's time to get to this decision about staying or leaving, but first let's rewind to the many choices that led to this moment in Haiti. I had found my decisions being increasingly affected by two stories: The first is Jesus with the rich young man. And there's a second story Jesus told that I couldn't get out of my head.

A rich man dies and goes to hell. From there the rich man begs Abraham (apparently the keeper of the gate before Peter) to send over a poor man named Lazarus from heaven to put a soothing drop of water on the rich man's burning tongue. On earth the poor man had lain outside the rich man's gate. Dogs licked his sores as he lay there scrounging for crumbs, while the rich man feasted sumptuously. Sorry, says Abraham, no can do. It's role reversal now.

I heard this parable for many years and was unbothered by it. Sure, those millionaire-billionaire people are feasting in their towering homes, with luxury toys, with diversified accounts full of money. Sure, it's wrong when others are barely surviving in poverty. But growing up middle-class in South Florida, my attention was drawn to those who were richer than we were. Other families had boats or backyard pools, and we didn't. My friends were given cars when they turned sixteen, and I wasn't.

Then my eyes and my chest opened, and it became frighteningly clear: that story is mine. I'm the rich man, not worthy of a drop of water on my tongue. Though nobody would consider me rich in my country, outside the gates it's a different story. And the parable's conclusion and definition of justice don't offer much latitude or easy hope: Abraham tells the rich man it's useless to send a warning back to his family members who haven't yet died, because they wouldn't change their ways to pay attention to those suffering beyond the gates anyway. They would, in essence, walk away, like the rich young man who came to Jesus.

But Jesus doesn't seem to agree with Abraham's pessimism. In telling the story, isn't he hoping we might change, might awaken to how much is at stake *right now?* Quite a warning and an invitation—to try both changing the world and finding salvation.

FLIGHT TO HAITI

It was one of our worst fights. Shelly was ready to be engaged; I was in love but hesitant. She was going on hikes with mutual friends while I stayed home going over a book about war and extreme deprivation by photojournalist James Nachtwey.

I'd returned from working with a refugee ministry for two years after college, met Shelly toward the end of seminary in Princeton, started dating her, returned to work in Albania and Kosovo for six months, then moved back to Princeton so I could be close to her. I took a good job but was left feeling numb because I didn't know what to do with those other feelings and conversations and experiences, like pushing a wheelbarrow beside someone who had lost everything else in the world except what was in that wheelbarrow.

I wanted to marry Shelly, but she hadn't met the same people I had. She didn't feel the same pull—though she was open. I didn't know how to say it to her, but how could I start down a path that could lead to a string of numbing jobs and binding mortgages and decisions based on what you have to do rather than what you believe in? Without giving myself any of the credit monastics deserve for their seriousness and without ever considering it as a possibility for myself, I felt like I needed to commit to all or nothing because I'm so weak and lazy that if I didn't enter a monastic-like promise of poverty and service sworn to the Almighty, if it wasn't marked daily by an itchy, rough-hewn robe with no pockets to keep anything in, then I was destined to constant compromise.

So I made a bumbling effort to say all this in what felt like a sensitive, honest way to the woman I loved and might want to marry, as we sat talking one afternoon in a room at our friends' place in upstate New York.

"Okay," she said. "So you want to get married. But first you need to solve all the great existential and practical questions of the world? Well at least that gives me a timeline." Then she threw a couch pillow at me. Then she cried. I felt like an idiot but still wasn't sure what to do.

Later she said, "If you're serious about this, then we do it together. No, I'm not drawn in exactly the same direction as you. But I'm open. And we believe in the same things. Can't you see that others do these things together and they're both stronger for it?" Her tone revealed that she was asking a dimwit.

We married a year later, and joyfully. But it did become more complicated. I was increasingly unhappy with not being engaged in these other bigger issues. Shelly had taken just a few short trips out of the country, but never to a place like Haiti, and never to live. After two years of conversations, prayers, occasional frustrations and dreaming, we made our way to the decision to move to Haiti.

My parents thought we were doing something relatively normal, if also worrisome for—and reason for much prayer by—my mom. Shelly's family wondered (at least it seemed to me) why their daughter had married a fool. Her dad had grown up in rural poverty after his own father died when he was twelve. He'd joined the army, become the North Dakota state prison warden and was respected around the state, rode bulls in an annual rodeo (okay, at least he wasn't completely sane), directed a ranch for at-risk youth, and expected one to always make judicious, long-vision decisions. Their conclusion wasn't quite this, but almost: I was taking their daughter away in pursuit of laudable ideals that should have been quenched with a Peace Corps stint after college; rather, I should be faithful to God in more sensible ways and take care of my family and the people I have direct responsibility for.

Foolish to chase ideals, but foolish not to. Foolish to take Jesus' stories seriously, but foolish not to. Foolish to let love be redefined by Jesus, who says you have no family, but everyone is your family. I had to give chase.

Twelve years earlier I had attended a Christian college in downtown West Palm Beach, Florida. I quickly became a business economics major. In my sophomore year I worked with a professor's help to resuscitate and become president of the campus business fraternity for two years. (It was our only fraternity of any type; this Southern Baptist–rooted school was no University of Florida.) Among the guests we invited to campus to speak and have lunch with us was a boss of The Breakers, one of the best-known luxury hotels in the world, which was just across the intracoastal on Palm Beach. We got along well, and I even took a girl on a date to watch him play polo.

I usually went to church. Occasionally I went with my youth group leader to give out food to guys who lived on the street downtown. But I was more serious about becoming successful in business. Until a kind of prophet showed up.

He appeared at one of our mandatory chapel services, which also featured American Free Enterprise Day once a year. In this picturesque First Baptist Church, suddenly there was a speaker up there making us laugh with his stories and then asking everyone—including this president of the business fraternity—"Can you really be a Christian and own a BMW?" (Good luck driving that through the eye of a needle.)

He told about a student who came to him excited because he just landed a plum job for which there had been hundreds of applicants. The speaker replied, "Why would you take a job that 199 other people could do when there's so much work Jesus is calling us to that nobody is doing?" These are basic Christian questions, but they're seldom asked. His way of communicating them upended presumptions I was starting to work with. The grace, anger and love in his message kicked some new life into me.

～

In the years leading up to the decision to move to Haiti, part of what helped me wade through the guilt and hypocrisy was not pretending—to myself and to others—that it's pure altruism. Rather, I could be honest about searching for more meaning but also committed to the hard work of making a better life possible for someone else.

So then one tries to follow Jesus by squeezing through the eye of the needle . . . and then stumbling outside the gates. Spending time there. Finding people we'd normally be asked to have mercy on—and instead asking them to have mercy on us and teach us.

There are all kinds of ways of helping that I admire, but I'm drawn to the more extreme. Maybe it's like a diet: it's usually easier for me either to drink three Cokes a day or decide I'm not going to drink any Coke for an entire year. Reasonable limits don't work best for me. And it's true in my trying to follow Jesus too. I relate to the young man slumping away from Jesus' demand for everything, but I'm also profoundly drawn to Jesus' radical demands. They strike me as true. They're so hard, yet I long for the invitation. At this intersection it seems grace, work, freedom, obedience, sacrifice and joy meld into a simple, whispered invitation.

But then what kind of narcissistic, messianic, self-important, desperate thing is this—or am I? Sure, some heroes like Saint Francis and Mother Teresa do a radical separation so they can go further into the world, but they're saints, and they're a bit nuts, and I'm pretty sure not everyone is supposed to do it their way. I always find more courage to do what I believe or want to believe when I'm not alone. Shelly's the one I wanted to be with me. Here she was, married to and loving a fool—and wanting, like me, to learn more about love. So we drive to the airport. We board the plane for Haiti.

There is an old missionary couple sitting one row up, across the aisle from us. We joke in whispers about hoping we aren't now en route to becoming like them: she has a doily-type thing on her head, and their clothes and demeanor give a heavy, stale impression. Then when we land on the Port-au-Prince runway, the old couple stands up to get their carry-ons. As they wait to disembark, we're behind them. Shelly nudges me and nods her head downward. The old man's hand is subtly—but provocatively—cupping his wife's bottom. Shelly and I smile at each other. We're a little anxious, but we're together. We walk out of the airplane door and blink into the sunlight, our eyes trying to adjust as we descend the metal stairs.

2

Getting (Dis)Oriented on the Other Side

THIRTY

This morning Shelly and I lie under a mosquito net and whisper as pigeons scratch and coo on the corrugated tin roof. Cocks crow, mangy dogs bark and a grandmother with a tattered dress and a nine-tooth smile sweeps fallen mango leaves from the ground just outside our door. The ecstatic drumbeats from an all-night Vodou fete had stopped. The seven insect bites on my ankles itch, and I worry the mosquitoes might have injected into my bloodstream lymphatic filarial parasites (tiny worms, basically) that would trigger the extreme enlargement and deformation of my scrotum—a malady apparently not uncommon in this region.

Today, a Friday in January 2003, I turn thirty. We've been here for a couple of weeks since first landing in Port-au-Prince and then, twenty-four hours later, settling into this eight-by-ten-foot room with a bed, chair, small table, gas lamp and a three-gallon water filter. The room is one of four in a square concrete house that we share with three generations of a Haitian family. The decorations they've provided for us include a calendar with slinky pop star Shakira in leather pants holding a Pepsi, and two identical cloth prints of a porcelain-skinned Jesus with reddish hair holding a tiny lamb.

Minutes after stepping outside this morning, I hear activity in a nearby field and walk over. Laughing boisterously, a neighbor named Frefre hands me his six-foot-long hoe, its smooth handle made from a tree branch. Suddenly I am working in a farm field for the first time in my life, preparing holes that would receive three seeds of *pwa konni* (a type of bean). With each swing, the soft skin of my hands feels a harsh, rewarding tug.

I return home for breakfast prepared by Grandma and the two sisters: coffee ground by mortar and pestle, and spaghetti noodles with a thin, oily tomato sauce. I give my last bites to Frefre's nephew, an eleven-year-old boy named David who had just helped teach me how to swing a hoe. All food is shared here, the plates passed around during a meal until family, friends and even animals have eaten.

After breakfast I accept from Frefre two plump *fransik* mangoes: a thank-you, I think, for my clumsy labor in his field. Wearing only a blue-and-white-checked school shirt, a rambunctious four-year-old boy sprints past with his penis bouncing merrily along. He is going to fetch a gallon of water at a pump a hundred yards down the dirt path. He's the second-youngest member of the family we're staying with. Their yard (called a *lakou*) is a quarter acre of dirt and pebbles with many tropical trees—coconut, mango, lime and others. Lush shades of green give the illusion of prosperity.

In addition to the concrete main house, the *lakou* has a second house of woven wood and an outhouse of palm leaves. Six turkeys, three chickens, two roosters and four guinea hens peck away incessantly in search of seeds. Tied to the trees are a goat and a calf, which I'm told serve as investments or insurance policies, to be sold when money is tight. Two dogs and a cat hover at mealtimes. The family includes a grandfather, grandmother, two adult daughters, a son-in-law, an adult niece, four grandchildren between four and twelve years old who belong to daughters living elsewhere, and the niece's baby.

Woshdlo, our tiny village, is a few hours outside Port-au-Prince. We chose to come with Beyond Borders largely because of this first requirement of living in a rural Haitian community as learners. Then we can integrate into the organization's work in education, literacy, teacher training and children's rights—supporting Haitians' efforts to improve their own lives. I've had enough experience elsewhere to know too many organizations and missions consist of foreigners coming in with the power to make decisions about people's lives before knowing anything. This way is more humble and realistic—and interesting. Hopefully it pays off in the long run with better understanding and thus more effective helping. But right now the intense, thorough immersion leaves little time for reflection. Though at least once a day something I see jolts me to think, *I can't believe how poor they are.*

Late this morning Frefre invites me to help him take a small bull to get water, and I keep control of the animal though it pulls me through a muddy canal. Then I take his large female cow (with horns) to get water. When the cow suddenly starts running, I sprint to keep up, yanking futilely on the rope. Frefre starts screaming something to me in Creole. I can't understand and have no idea whether releasing his cow will send it on a child-maiming rampage, lose the cow forever, or be perfectly logical and harmless. The rope is burning my hands and the cow is running too fast for me to keep up, so I have no choice but to hope his cries of "*Lage l! Lage l!*" mean "Let it go! Let it go!"

The story dashes through the village. I soon begin showing my palms to any who want to see how trying to rein in a runaway cow affects soft pink hands. I don't mind. Five hundred years ago Africans began to be imported to this island to bear the burns and calluses and burdens while soft pink hands counted the profits.

Back at the house, Shelly gives me a tin coffee cup for my birthday—to drink our filtered water—along with a card that she'd decorated with drawings of everyone we live with, including the animals.

⌒

Lunch is dense, boiled plantains covered in another oily sauce with a few small chunks of beef. This area has relatively rich soil and adequate water. People are poor and struggling, but when the weather is right and there aren't any blights, they get by with their crops of sugar cane, corn, beans and plantains. But some families don't have good garden plots, and it's not hard to imagine a time when the rains won't come. When that happens, the people here in this area would be poor *and* hungry, like many other Haitians.

After lunch a middle-aged woman walks by on the path, a large *kivet* overflowing with provisions balanced atop her head. She is barefoot and wearing an attractive though slightly ragged cream-colored dress, cut just below the knee and not zipped up all the way in back. I imagine the dress being given to a secondhand store years ago by an American businesswoman. Used-clothing imports can make for funny juxtapositions, like a woman carrying a heavy load of vegetables on her head to the market in the hot sun, sweating profusely, wearing a shirt that says "It's a Hunny of a Day" under a broadly smiling Winnie the Pooh. The Haitian woman in the dress doesn't look funny, though. I can't imagine the dress looking more beautiful on anyone else.

Woshdlo has received us with a generosity, warmth and patience that we find somewhat embarrassing, considering our own country's inhospitality toward Haitians. By chance, the day I resigned from my job in Princeton to move here, the *New York Times* featured a front-page photo of some of the two hundred Haitians who had just survived a hazardous trip to Florida's coast on a rickety boat, only to be detained like prisoners to await being sent back to the very situation they were fleeing.

Not that everyone in Haiti has offered us a warm welcome. As we walk down the muddy paths and roads, we often hear cries of *"Blan!"* which literally means "white" but also refers to any foreigner. People say it with curiosity or derision—or a mix of the two. Yet pale skin can just as easily open doors to special privileges. Last night two guys told me that one of their nation's founding fathers was ugly because his skin was so dark—"triple blackout black." The elite in Haiti have typically been mulatto. This afternoon, however, the same two spoke derisively of an albino Haitian because he was *blan.* Each time *"Blan!"* is hurled my way, I feel vaguely ashamed and embarrassed. My weak return volley is

"My *name* is Kent. What's yours?"

This afternoon I invite Frefre, whose field I had worked in this morning, to play a card game I'd just been taught called *kazino*. He is wearing a black, hole-riddled Orlando Predators T-shirt—the only shirt I've seen him wear. The rules of the card game are simple: if you have an eight in your hand, and there's an eight on the table, you put the two eights in your pile. But he doesn't catch on. The other guys tease him. I feel bad. While we are playing, he asks if I have blisters from this morning's work in his field. Then he shows me his hands. They are like leather, cured by a lifetime of farming with hoe and machete. At the end of the game he counts his cards—slowly and not altogether accurately—to twenty-nine.

Frefre has no education, can't read or write or even—as I just awkwardly learned—count well. But he has something I envy: quiet confidence in his work. He knows exactly what he needs to do each day and does it skillfully.

We sit outside after finishing the card game. The kids are playing and doing chores. They go to school in the mornings—when it's in session and there's no teachers' strike. In the afternoons they have little supervision and regularly play with fire and machetes. It isn't uncommon to see the four-year-old boy we live with dash by with a plastic bag over his head and a machete in his hand, after playing with the cooking fire. From what I hear, it would be normal for children to be punished occasionally with a switch, though I haven't seen that happen in our Woshdlo family.

I was quickly drawn to these children. They love to sing and dance and tell stories. They've taught me the Creole words for all the vegetation and animals. They daily fetch countless gallons of water. When I accidentally broke one of their toys, a small piece of discarded plastic, the seven-year-old tried for a few minutes to fix it and then ran off to find something else to play with. A dozen rusting D-size batteries, perhaps.

But the four-year-old, the most aggressively curious and hardworking child I've ever met, can't count to three. The seven-year-old, a charming schemer, can barely sound out words in a book. When he does read, it's to memorize passages from a 1968 textbook written in French—a language he doesn't really understand and likely won't ever have reason to speak. (The echoes of colonialism are difficult to silence.)

We haven't faced anything truly heartbreaking yet, at least among our immediate acquaintances. But during a tour at the nearest hospital, which I'm told is among the best in Haiti, I heard the receptionist telling mothers with sick children, "Come back tomorrow, and maybe you'll get to see a doctor, si Dye vle"—"God willing." That is attached to the end of any statement about the future, whether plans for a meeting tomorrow morning or the harvest in three months. In this place the phrase seems alternately a statement of stark fatalism, a bitter taunt directed toward the Divine or the most unsentimental confession of faith I've ever heard.

We're quickly coming to care deeply about Grandmother, Grandfather, the daughters, son-in-law, grandchildren, Frefre, David and others we've met. A faint nausea has settled in my stomach—the fear that one of them will become severely ill. Whoever it is won't get airlifted to Miami, as I would.

After fetching some water at the source, we sit back on the porch. A man walks by wearing only shorts and carrying a machete in his hand. His body is gleaming and beautiful, each muscle sinuous and hard. My various anxieties about living in Haiti have distilled to two potent fears: mosquito-borne illnesses and imagined threats to Shelly. This culture is more openly sexually aggressive than ours, and the looks men give her, along with their unsheathed machetes and the strength of their bodies, don't calm my fears.

At dusk Shelly and I walk with members of the family through the sugar-cane fields into town. The sunset is beautiful through the coconut and mango trees, and a gigantic full moon hangs waiting at the other end of the sky. Later we make our way home through the dark, puddle-filled streets. A few vendors remain open, selling fried bread or candies, with their small stands dimly lit by candles. I count these as my birthday candles. The life expectancy for Haitian males—with infant mortality, AIDS and poverty working their cruel subtraction—is fifty-one years. Not too many candles away.

After arriving home, we sit outside under the bright moon with the family. Grandfather says, as he has every day, "I put in a hard day's work again today. All day long. Hard, hard work. I have to work all the time." And he does work hard: I've seen him planting seeds by hoe and scaling a fifty-foot coconut tree with his bare hands and feet. But his lament feels forced. Maybe he thinks we can provide access to America's wealth. A Haitian we've befriended has told us that, whether they admit it or not, "All Haitians think this way." I don't believe this is true, though I don't doubt it would be true of me, were our circumstances reversed.

Despite Grandfather's impulse to impose his patriarchal will (particularly by making Shelly eat piles of rice), he is positioning himself to receive our help, because he imagines we hold some power over him. We hold the keys to the kingdom. Everyone is using everyone else, it seems. We're using the family's hospitality to learn the language and the culture; the son-in-law uses us to show off to his friends; the grandfather uses us as an investment toward a future payoff.

This might seem cynical, but it's just real life. Cynical charity uses innocent kids and preposterous statements about changing the world for loose change—nothing else required of you. Real charity, the kind that does more than just relieve one's conscience, is more complex, more demanding. I vacillate between despair—*how could we possibly be of any use here?*—and trust that we're in the right place, for the right reasons, with the right people, and whatever comes of it will be for the better.

While we continue talking with Grandfather under the stars and moon, the neighborhood children gather to sing and dance and play musical chairs. I get up and dance around the chairs for a while. During a break I drink a mixture of juice and milk cooled by an ice cube that may contain parasites that will make me sick. It tastes great and would have been awkward to refuse. I check the time, and immediately a circle of young boys surround me and make me light the Indiglo dial of my watch again and again. Then I go to the outdoor shower at the back of the concrete house and, with a yellow margarine container, scoop water out of a large bucket to wash away the day's grime. The water is cold, and the moonlight shines brilliantly through the fifteen-foot-long banana leaves fanned out overhead. I never envisioned myself here at thirty, but there's no place else I would rather be today.

After saying *bon nwit* to everyone, I go to my room. Shelly is already asleep under the mosquito net. Staticky dance music plays on the radio in the next room; the newlywed daughter and son-in-law turn it up each night to partially cover their urgent breathing.

As I fall asleep, I occasionally jerk awake to gasp for air. This started a few days ago, like a sudden onset of sleep apnea. It's unsettling. Irrationally I wonder if someone put a curse on the new *blans* in town.

Drifting further into sleep, I think of Shelly, who by request earlier in the evening had acted out for the tenth time, with her few Creole words, how I was pulled through the field by the cow while Frefre yelled, *"Lage l! Lage l!" "Let go! Let go!"* After she was finished, I asked one of the family's relatives whether a cow had ever pulled him like that. He laughed and said, "All the time." I seem to be laughing with less restraint than during the past several years in Princeton, though of course it's far from all being happy or easy.

STRIKES

We leave our house early to walk twenty minutes to the nearby town so I can catch the tap-tap. A tap-tap is a small, covered pickup truck painted in festive colors that serves as a bus and crams a seemingly impossible fourteen to sixteen people in the back. Shelly and I part in the chaotic outdoor market. She goes back home to help the family with chores. Our Creole is improving, and we're moving with a little more confidence. I walk to where charcoal is sold, just past where Madam Sylvanie squats all day under her umbrella-size straw hat selling salt, to catch the ride that takes twenty washboard minutes to get to Léogane, the nearest city. I wait with a group in the shade. After five minutes, a girl says, "No rides today. There's a strike because the gas price is too high." I talk with her and her friends for a few minutes. In a place where logistics can drive you crazy, you have to roll with the circumstances. But I'm not yet willing to completely surrender my desire to get things done when I want them done, so I start walking.

A month before we arrived in Haiti, the tap-tap to Léogane had cost three gouds (seven cents), and now, just six weeks after being here, it costs seven gouds. Prices of other basic provisions keep rising too. Middle- and even working-class Americans can trim their budgets during most systemic or personal financial slowdowns; people here don't have many options. The sisters in our family walk to the Léogane market instead of riding the tap-tap to save seven gouds each. Nana stops giving her kids money to buy candy to save four gouds. People forgo a weekly Coke or Sprite that costs twelve gouds for a half-liter.

It is already hot. Halfway along the dusty road that hasn't seen rain in two weeks, a commotion erupts a hundred feet ahead. Two trucks and a tap-tap full of people skid to a stop. Dust kicks up. People are running around the vehicles and yelling. I slow, stop, watch. Then men start throwing rocks, and more young men join them. I turn and start back in the opposite direction. My skin makes me stand out; I figure standing out isn't a good idea near an angry mob. Some women with baskets of food on their heads had stopped too, and they tease me for not wanting to continue on: "Look, the *blan* doesn't want to keep going up there!"

"Of course not," I laugh, as I keep walking in the opposite direction, resigned that another day would have to do. Then a young man I'd never met before, who is standing beside his bike with books in his hands, says, "Come on. We'll use the inner route. They're mad because a tap-tap is breaking the strike." I hesitate, then follow.

We detour through paths and fields. He is a student in his last year of high school. We talk about Kobe, Shaq and Iverson. He talks about how hard times are, how everyone who isn't a farmer is unemployed, how everyone who can is leaving the country. His mom and dad live in Guadeloupe. He put some blame on the politicians. He would like to visit the United States; it looks nice on TV. We talk and walk for an hour. I have no idea where we are amid the tall stalks of sugar cane and corn, but then we appear in Léogane.

We wish each other a good day. Then for a couple of hours I sit in front of one of the dozen dusty computers that line the walls of a little Internet room run by Allan, a twenty-five-year-old who wants to be a rapper and whose self-given nickname is DJ Action. A single fan rotates. The latest Eminem song blasts as a French nun types e-mails, a young Haitian woman works on her resume, two teenage Haitian guys click through close-up pictures of two black men having sex with a white woman, a young Mormon missionary plays FreeCell, and I type e-mails. Later I'll figure out how to get back.

⌒

Sandra was the first person outside the family we're living with to take us under her wing. Other than Frefre, who had quickly welcomed me into his field, people were initially friendly and curious, but reticent too. Sandra took Shelly on walks to the market to learn how to shop and around town to meet women friends.

Then this morning her husband comes walking down the path in a bad mood—angrily punching the air and talking loudly to himself. I ask what is wrong. He says someone had stolen seven plantain trees out of his field the night before, presumably to feed their cows. "My friend, times are getting hard," he sputters. "It's getting dangerous here. People just don't have enough." He seems as upset with the overall situation as with the thief.

Later in the morning we stop to talk with Sandra, who is sitting on their porch, pumping her feet up and down on her manual sewing machine as she makes a dress for a neighbor. Like several other women nearby, she can't afford to buy crackers and candies to sell in town anymore, so sewing is all she has left. But she can barely earn any money from that either, since local tailors have been undercut by used-clothing donations shipped from the United States and sold cheaply in the outdoor markets.

Then this afternoon we hear yelling and then shrieks at their house. Then a slapping noise, again and again. We freeze. Grandmother dashes by with Grandfather quickly following her. A few kids sprint to catch the action. Others are already on the scene, so we stay put. We're still new guests and don't want to presume too much on entering people's lives. Only when invited.

Then Andrelita, the fighting couple's three-year-old granddaughter, starts down the path toward us, away from the fight. She is barefoot and wearing a frilly red dress. She takes a few tentative steps, crouches down, looks back over her shoulder toward the commotion, then keeps walking down the path toward our house. Pause. Crouch. Look back. Take a few more of her little steps. Shelly and I call out, *"Vini. Vini isit."*—"Come here." She had been scared of us to this point, usually turning away and refusing to let us come too near, but now she sprints straight into my arms. She stays there for a couple hours after the dispute quiets, eventually falling asleep. By then family members and friends drift back, telling us that Sandra's husband (stolen plantain trees) and Sandra had started fighting verbally over money and school tuition for their kids. At some point it turned physical. She wielded her sewing scissors. He overpowered her and beat her until neighbors pulled him off. Grandmother proudly shows off the cut on her hand from yanking the scissors out of his hand. Shelly and I sit in the *lakou*, feeling sad and talking with the family.

For the past few weeks we had watched as these two good people were squeezed—as if in slow motion—until today, when they exploded at each other, which will only make the situation worse for themselves and their children. The way systemic problems like global economics and gas prices ripple out to this place is brutal. OPEC price hikes and global market trends are suddenly intensely personal. The aphorism "Pull yourself up by the bootstraps" comes ironically to mind because it's so inapplicable: if you can't afford boots, don't have any power and barely any resources, if there's no way to hoist yourself up, then when you need something (say, food or tuition for your kids) the choices are either to ask for it or take it. Or suffer quietly. Or throw rocks at a tap-tap or hit your wife. So are good, brilliant, powerful people working somewhere to find systemic economic and political solutions to the problems we see crushing down on our neighbors? And will the good guys win? Because too often they don't.

Shelly and I keep shucking beans for tomorrow's meal—feeling reassured by Grandmother, who is sitting next to us shucking with her bandaged hand, strangely grateful that Andrelita chose to sleep here on my lap, and more than a little helpless. Is it supposed to work this way, that the more we learn and integrate, the farther apart our lives feel? Can we really connect across this chasm—divided by language, passports, history, money?

US. THEM.

"So, can we come in?"

"Yes, come in, come in! They're finally coming in the house! We thought you'd never come in. We thought you didn't want to visit us in this house, but wanted to stay in your part of the concrete house."

"But we didn't know if we were supposed to come in, or should wait to be invited."

"Look, Kent. This is where I sleep."

"Shelly, Shelly, this is where the three of us sleep."

"Over here, over here, I'm in this bed with Grandpa and Grandma."

Grandmother is in her bed, propped on one elbow, watching with a mischievous smile. Grandfather, Grandmother, four of the five grandchildren and occasional extended family members sleep in this house.

"Grandma was just going to tell a story. Tell her to tell the vwazen djab *story."*

"No, not that one. I want her to do one with a song."

We've sat in a circle in the yard sometimes as Grandmother told stories, and sometimes we could hear her from inside this second house with thatched walls and mud floor. She rolls out of bed slowly. Grandmother's left leg has been swollen and aching, but she has an audience to please.

⌒

Along with some Haitian friends and an American colleague,

Shelly and I traveled in a van for ten jarring hours from our village to Cap-Haïtien, a city on Haiti's northern coast—a nice way to see more of the country and make a brief escape from the confines of the village. After three months it can feel suffocating at times, but we can also communicate more, understand more and enjoy developing friendships.

While in Cap-Haïtien, we hiked up to see the Citadel, an imposing fortress built two centuries ago by the nation's second leader, Henri Christophe, to ward off any future attacks by the French colonists who had just been expelled. As we walked back down after our visit, we saw small pockets of chaos scattered around the parking lot. Ah yes, North Americans! It started harmlessly enough as the visitors haggled for trinkets. Then one woman started giving out small gifts such as candy and key chains to the Haitians she met. Of course, soon everyone wanted to meet her.

A crowd encircled the woman. The reaching hands rapidly grew more numerous than her gifts. With her bag empty, she reached into her pockets and started handing out money. The crowd grew bigger still. It was time for her to leave, and, overwhelmed, she climbed onto the back of her group's flatbed truck. Yet even as the truck started moving away, the hands kept beckoning, and the crowd began pursuing. Moved by the clamorous need, her bag and pockets now empty, the woman reached to her neck, took off her necklace and threw it into the crowd, which triggered undignified scrambling, minor brawling and ever louder cries for more gifts, more money, more jewelry. It was charity fit to incite a riot.

The next day our Haitian friends wanted to go to Labadie beach, which they'd all heard was where the cruise ships stop. It felt like a setup for penance: only one of the four Haitian men had been to the United States and so had any idea of the kind of luxury we might see.

We arrived at the secluded beach after winding through narrow mountain roads. A behemoth ship floated like an alien craft out on the sea. Its price tag could buy how much of this country? Near the glaring white ship, people ate on the beach, played on big water toys such as trampolines and roared around on WaveRunners. And I almost ran into an angry, stone-throwing mob a couple of months ago because tap-tap prices had increased from seven to seventeen cents? How many barrels of gas were my compatriots burning here by the minute? Together we watched through a chainlink fence. It's new for me to watch from this side of the fence. Eventually we took a short boat ride to a beautiful, quiet beach not far away. It was a relief to be out of sight of the ship that emphasized the glaring divides between us—and then to dive together into the warm blue Caribbean Sea.

⌒

Back in the village a couple of weeks after the trip, the glow of an evening fire illuminated the *lakou*. Garbage time. The burning pile consisted mostly of fallen leaves swept together by Grandma during the day, but it included some trash as well. There's almost no paper or plastic waste generated by our family; you have to buy lots to waste lots. One of the kids runs to a neighbor's house every day with the same little plastic container to buy enough cooking oil or tomato paste for that afternoon's meal. A hotel-size bottle is refilled every few days with shampoo bought from a different neighbor, who sells from a big jug. Shelly and I had some tissue and small scraps of paper to throw in the fire.

Though we've been here a few months, we're still a mystery, so a small group wandered over to watch as I took things out of a small plastic bag and threw them into the flames. Used tissues— no big deal. An empty box of prunes (for trying to help our bodies digest the piles of starch) hit a branch and bounced out. One of the neighbor boys picked it up, examined it, tossed it back into the fire. More scraps, tissues. Then I threw a glossy, full-spread pull-out advertisement from an issue of *Rolling Stone* that a colleague had given us (we're happy for anything English to read). The ad was, I think, for a VH1 music special, a Robert Plant album and other music stuff; it was an annoyance in the magazine. As it landed in the fire, David, the boy who had taught me how to swing a hoe on my birthday, dashed to rescue it despite the risk of singeing his skin.

Soon everyone was gathering around. We watched a little uncomfortably. Had they never seen anything with print quality that good? Several times they've shown me with pride the few low-quality color photos in one of their textbooks. Children and adults looked intently at Robert Plant, though they didn't understand the English captions.

Eventually David retook possession and meticulously folded the ad into a little square. With a big smile, he walked over and told me he would put it in his backpack—which, other than the few clothes that he bunches together as a makeshift mattress for sleeping on the concrete floor, might be the only thing he owns. "It's special," he said. "Sometimes I can take it out and look at it, and it will make me happy." As I told Shelly what he had just said, my voice cracked. A useless scrap generated by our culture's hype machine is special to this eleven-year-old child. He very deliberately put his new treasure in his pocket.

Some travel writers and organizations like ours use childhood as a metaphor for crossing into a new culture. That works to an extent; there's curiosity, the fun and frustration of discovery, and a certain helpless reliance on others. But it's childhood without innocence, which is a tainted childhood. Presumed upon. Demanded from. I know a little something about the history between my race and theirs—and so do they. Imbalance of money and power fundamentally changes relationships.

After we were communicating better, the son-in-law in our family retold the joke he had told—which we hadn't understood—at our community welcome party the first night we arrived: "On Judgment Day, Jesus separated the good from the bad on his right and left. To the right he put all the presidents of the world and sent them to hell. They all had cell phones and wanted to call home from hell, but couldn't get a signal, so went to a pay phone. The president of France asks, 'How much for a two-minute call back home to France?' 'Twenty thousand francs,' says hell's pay-phone steward. After the French president finishes talking, the American president asks, 'How much to call the U.S. for five minutes?' 'Fifty thousand dollars,' says the steward. Then the Haitian president says, with some reluctance, that he isn't sure how much time he needs. He asks if he can just go ahead and call, and then pay afterward. He has lots of people to talk with, so the call goes on for two hours. After he hangs up, he asks the steward how much. 'Four gouds,' says the steward (about ten cents). Confused, the Haitian president asks if the price is correct and demands an explanation. The steward explains, 'Haiti's a local call from here.'" Uproarious laughter had followed. Welcome to Haiti.

Haitians know their place in the hierarchy of nations, especially compared with the Hulking Neighbor a ninety-minute flight to the north. The Great Neighbor recently went to war in Iraq. Teenage boys sometimes ask about the war as we sit in the shade on a fallen palm tree, but they know more than I do about how it's progressing. I can't yet keep up with the radio's rapid Creole news reports.

Our conversation shifts to the September 11 attacks. A couple of them express admiration for Osama bin Laden. I'm angry. Three thousand innocent people died, including the husband of someone I had worked with in Princeton. Yet it's obvious they are sympathetic because someone had revealed a little chink in the armor of King Kong (us), who has stomped on Haiti (them) more than once and who decides what to give as everyone else braces to receive. Out here in the village, they somehow feel better knowing the eight-hundred-pound gorilla is vulnerable too.

~

Everyone sits on two single beds, with Grandmother down at one end. The four-year-old has cuddled onto Shelly's lap. The room is lit by a tiny lamp with gas in the tin base and a small wick that keeps an inch-long flame flickering. This afternoon's cold, leftover rice and beans is making the round in a tin bowl. We've tended to retire to our room, tired from the day's stimuli, earlier than the family each night, so we haven't known this part of the routine. The seven-year-old is whispering story requests into my ear, figuring if I convey them to Grandmother he'll have a better shot at hearing his favorite.

Finally, Grandmother says in the near dark, "There was a neighbor in a little town who was a djab *[a kind of evil spirit] . . ."*

Soon she is singing and dancing on the packed-dirt floor—hopping in a circle as she jabs the sky rhythmically with her right hand, her left hand supporting her right elbow. The story is spoken, but there's an occasional chorus that everyone sings together.

Grandfather comes in and says, "You're finally in here listening to her stories." I ask about his day. "Planted some corn. Now I'll sleep a few hours, then go water the garden by moonlight."

The seven-year-old on my lap says, "Grandpa isn't even scared of the spirits. Nobody else will go water alone at night."

Grandfather shrugs. "I don't have to be scared of the spirits. Jesus will protect me."

Sounds like one of the evil spirits in Grandmother's story just ate a child. The wordplay and cultural references are far beyond my understanding, but I love hearing her stories. Especially the ones with songs

that everyone joins in on. The four-year-old is asleep in Shelly's arms.
The seven-year-old has rolled over to lie down behind me. One of the
sisters has gone back to her room in the concrete house ten feet away,
where our room is. Grandmother is performing for us now, though I
have no idea what the plot is.

⌒

Our citizenship and shiny skin give us a weird kind of celebrity.
One day a kid we barely know ran up to Shelly in our village, panting and excited, and said, "I saw Kent last Tuesday morning! He
was at the bus station in Léogane, walking toward the center of
town. He had just bought an orange-flavored juice and three plantain patties!" An oral version of *People* magazine, I guess.

Then recently when I was waiting outside in line to use a pay
phone, a young, well-dressed woman I'd never seen before was
just in front of me in the line and asked me for money. When I
said, "Sorry, no," she laid into me in front of a bunch of people,
calling me "cheap" and "hard" and other names I thankfully don't
yet understand. I stood, eyes down, waiting for the phone.

This is new for me: I grew up white and middle-class in mostly
white, middle-class neighborhoods. It's bizarre to evoke such re-
sponses simply by walking down the street—though of course it's
not just skin. It's a reminder of so much history. It's a reminder of
so much politics and economics and injustice—past and present.
And though our situations aren't parallel, it reminds me, of course,
of what many people still experience in my own country, whose
skin isn't the same color as mine.

I feel occasional resentment: Why do I have to fend off this
daily assault of need and requests when rich people back in the
States never have to deal with it so personally, so in-your-face, so
real, so everywhere? "Hey, at least I'm making an effort," I want to
say, pointing a finger into the aggressive asker's chest. "Go bother

the people lounging on the cruise ships! Or bother the people who don't even try to help!" But of course there's a chainlink fence to keep that from happening—and the Coast Guard patrolling the warm sea between here and Florida.

⌒

Trying to give through this fence, across this sea, is complicated. On birthdays we gave colorful stickers to the kids, which were a hit. We had a whole pack, but we just gave one sheet at a time since any more would have outshone the little gifts from others in the family. At the same time, they know we have access to more resources, and we don't want to be cheap.

We don't want to be seen simply as foreign patrons, reinforcing an unhealthy historic paternalism (combined with exploitation) that can lead to unhelpful relationships of dependency. We don't want to be seen primarily as giver-outers-of-stuff (whether food aid or cheap toys). But we also want to give everything we have, everything we could possibly get our hands on.

How to convey how complicated this feels? The "foreign aid" dynamic here is charged. I do know that when we've asked other long-term foreigners here for counsel, they've responded with phrases like "Good luck" or "Let me know if you find the answer."

Frefre introduced me to a friend of his, a kind, gentle, hardworking neighbor named Gardinal. He's about my age and has lost half his teeth already. The rest are blackening into stumps in his mouth. Why not take him to the dentist and pay for the best possible care? Well, then, would you do it for everyone else with problems as serious? Because if you helped one person, then it's guaranteed that the next day twenty people with problems as bad or worse would line up to talk with you. What about those with chronic stomach problems, or a million other genuine, pressing, painful problems? We can't afford to fix everything, and the needs go on and on. And then we know all of our relationships would instantly change because we'd be seen as a source for covering these expenses. Yes, but so what? Even if I can't change the world, I could at least help one guy who's on his way to being toothless by thirty-five. Okay, but what does it do to his relationships in the community? And does it reinforce a damaging cycle of relationships between Haitians and Americans that needs to be reinvented? Yes . . . but then there's just basic human need, and who cares about psychology, anthropology, sociology and history when a guy is suffering fifteen brutal cavities? The debate swirls in my head.

Then one day on the path, I see another neighbor, Wonald, and we chat while walking toward our village. He's walking home from his garden with eight ears of freshly picked corn in his hand, the husks tied together so they're easy to carry. Then with a smile, but without making a big deal of it, Wonald puts all of the corn in my hand, and waves off my genuine attempt to refuse the gift because it's the second time he's done this in three weeks.

And another time recently, Shelly and I piled into the tap-tap for the ride to Léogane. We ended up sitting across from an acquaintance. He's always friendly. I don't remember his name. We said hi to each other, then halfway through the trip, when it was time to pay the seven gouds each, he glanced timidly at us and quickly gave the collector twenty-one gouds. Pointing to himself, then Shelly and then me, he said, "For the three of us."

⌒

Grandmother sings the chorus and then concludes with a jumping flourish, "And he died!" The kids sleepily cheer the finale. It feels like—how to say this—like we're almost on sacred ground, I guess because we're here by grace, without having done anything to earn a welcome into moments like this, in this place.

Grandmother is laughing, and the twelve-year-old girl, who spent four straight hours this afternoon scrubbing dishes (as she does almost every day), props her head up and says, "So, did you understand the story?"

"Um, yes."

"All of it?"

"Well, lots of it."

"Not all?"

"Well, the idea, but my Creole can't understand it all yet."

Luckily she doesn't test me by asking for a synopsis. Grandmother slumps slightly at my answer. But she comes over to give us each a good-night kiss on the cheek, then walks to her single bed to wriggle in between the seven-year-old and Grandfather. Shelly is asleep next to the four-year-old. I rouse her to walk over to our room.

3

Giving Up and Finding

DESIRE

I want a Burger King bacon double cheeseburger. I want U2's *Achtung Baby* blasting my eardrums. I want to drive—as fast as I want, no potholes, windows down, turning where I please. I want to rent two new releases, grab some chips and salsa and a pint of Ben & Jerry's to fritter the night away. I want to pick up the phone and talk with my sister or brother. I want lightning-speed Internet. I want to nap on an ergonomically designed pillow with the air conditioner blasting frigid relief over me. I want to wander down to the bookstore to pick up the latest hardback by my favorite novelist. I want to listen to *Mike and the Mad Dog* on New York City sports talk radio. I want an SUV, four-by-four. I want five hundred channels beaming through my satellite. I want to meander along paved streets lined with gorgeous cherry blossoms. I want a job that I'm good at and recognized for. I want to eat dinner at our friends' place, afterward moving to the living room to have another glass of wine and talk till midnight. I want to lose myself in competition, basketball or racquetball or chess or anything. I want. I want. I want.

We've been living in Woshdlo for four months. Yesterday afternoon that occasional hollow, palpable ache opened in my chest—the ache that isn't healed by anything in the above paragraph but is certainly soothed by all of it.

I felt kind of helpless and impotent, a little lonely. I didn't know what to do or why it should be done, or even if I should find something to do. Moving across cultures this thoroughly means leaving behind many legitimate pillars of support, like relationships and language. It also means leaving behind the culture and convenient escapes that are so reliably useful to numb the mysterious ache that, for me at least, points toward God via the reality that life is disappointing and painful and incomplete.

Things on the above list aren't all bad. But part of why I looked forward to moving to Haiti is because I hate how easy it is to satiate my hunger for God and for good and for love by stuffing my appetites with food, with entertainment, with ambition, with stuff. How easy it is to fill the echo chamber that calls me toward God and good and love with other clanging noises. The absence in Haiti of choices to feed this profound hunger is unpleasant . . . but I need it. I'm too often too weak to hunger for good (or, to be more biblical, to seek the kingdom of God) and to pull away from the dancing lights that have embarrassing power over me, like over a mindless, fluttering moth.

So yesterday as I scuffed along in my flip-flops, with my head bent slightly forward and disconsolate, through Léogane's dusty streets, past the vendors selling fried plantains and used T-shirts, the emptiness ached—with no choices for soothing or numbing it—and I actually turned toward prayer. Prayer in turn led me to focusing on my neighbors instead of myself, which led me to thinking about and then later finding a way to do something small but tangible to improve the health of one of our young neighbors.

This is a confession of weakness, not an example of strength. If there's medication within reach to ease my spirit's distress, I'll grab and gulp. But I hate that this is my reflexive response. I'd rather love or reach for God—or even just feel the truth behind the ache.

—

Oh, and not to forget about the sexual aches. Actually, early in our stay here I realized—a nice surprise—that for six weeks I had not wanted sex with anyone other than my wife. Not with the perfect, airbrushed body on an *FHM* magazine cover in the airport. Not with the lithe heroine of last night's action movie. Not with the endless stream of perfect curves with pouty lips in commercials.

This, even though many women in our area are attractive and

partially naked. One sees more bare breasts on an average day in Woshdlo than in an issue of *Playboy*. You exchange *bonjou*s with a woman out bathing in her yard at dusk wearing only panties. You stop to chat with a neighbor, Nana, who, because it's so warm at midday, is wearing only a skirt as she hunches over a boiling pot of beans or as she rests on the porch. Adolescent neighbor girls, wrapped in towels but without much concern about whether they flap open, walk down the path to the nearest water source to bathe.

One night the sensuality around me—the skin, the fluid movement, the dancing—found form in a dream about Naomi Campbell. You can't expect all cultural images to dissipate immediately, I guess, but at least what fed my dream was something real: latent sexual tension from living in close quarters with people I've actually seen or greeted with a kiss on the cheek. Much of the lust that maneuvered its way from television or film or print into my mind so I would buy pizza or alcohol, movie tickets or toothpaste— much of its impersonal manipulation has vanished since I relocated to the poorest country in the Western Hemisphere.

So besides the generous hospitality, one welcome gift that I'm being given is shelter from the vicious consumer advertising storm that whips our North American culture—our individual psyches— into a whirlwind: consumer feeding corporation feeding politics feeding greed feeding consumer feeding corporation feeding politics feeding greed feeding . . .

Before we left the United States, I listened to NPR, avoided most TV and drove a Honda CRX with more than 200,000 miles on it. But desires are easily tossed by the winds of consumption. Before the flight to Haiti, a small part of my brain was occupied with when and how to see Leo DiCaprio's two new Christmas movies. I was disappointed about not getting a promotion—and would have welcomed the accompanying (albeit minimal) recognition and raise. I awaited each new episode of *The Sopranos* and didn't mind appearances of Adriana, with those legs, those skirts. I drank sixteen ounces of Dr. Pepper at two o'clock every afternoon.

Now I'm eating beans and rice or plantains every day. I don't own a bike—let alone a car—and though I'm still rich by Haitian standards, I'm earning a tenth of my previous salary. Neither super-sizing nor upgrading nor celebrities nor promotions have flitted across my brain.

Economic deprivation, as faced by the majority of Haitians, is not, of course, an alternative to consumer culture that I would choose for anybody. Coaxing enough food for your family from a small plot of depleted soil in Woshdlo, let alone slum dwelling, is not a romantic return to the Garden of Eden or "simplicity." But as an expatriate here, I have breathed more deeply since escaping the cynical, distracting pull of marketing. Stepping out of the dizzying whirlwind of false needs and false promises is, of course, possible in New York, Minneapolis, Vancouver or Austin. People are doing it. But it's harder there—hard to even realize the sheer force of what you're caught in—than here.

I've escaped sex as an all-powerful sales device, even as I find myself in what is, on the surface at least, a promiscuous culture—with open talk about multiple girlfriends and men's mistresses and second families. But at least it's between real people—not with airbrushed models, Internet porn stars or the latest manufactured pop plaything. And at night I lie in bed next to Shelly, with the warm tropical air making our skin slightly sticky where we touch.

⌒

Unfortunately, five months later, this freedom from the temptation of forbidden fruit hasn't unleashed transcendent Garden of Eden sex. For example, it's mid-afternoon—very hot outside and even hotter inside, with no windows, as the heat radiates down in palpable waves from the tin roof. Dough on our little table would turn to bread. I'm sick. I lie on the bed, sweating profusely, reading a book, searching vainly for sleep, hoping to tap a yet-undiscovered source of energy. Shelly comes in. We've already spent a good seven hours together during the day. She lies down right next to me on the bed. Maybe she was just being kind and wanting to see how I was, but maybe she was provoking me. So I mutter just loud enough, not with meanness but not with tender loving care, "Get away from me."

I wasn't being hostile. It was just too hot already, and her being close made it hotter. I had the energy to muster a maximum of four words, and "Get away from me" was the most efficient way to express "Leave me alone and take your body heat with you." No, these kinds of comments won't fast-track me into the Fantastic Husbands Hall of Fame. I've been on the receiving end too. It seems unavoidable with our marriage in this pressure cooker (or steamer or oven).

Physically, I'm beat. Emotionally, Shelly has found all this very strenuous. The culture here isn't gentle and doesn't fit well with her more tender personality. She's put her career on hold, and like me, she's going through the normal stresses of crossing cultures and languages. (Language learning has also been easier for me because I already knew some French, which has many similarities to Haitian Creole.) She sometimes cries herself to sleep. We get almost no time alone. Too often we just give each other the dregs, but it's not like I can speak English to everyone today because it's just too tiring to speak Creole and I'd rather save a little extra energy for Shelly.

Yet how incredible—and how grateful I am—to share this experience with her. I think Shelly feels this way too. Most days. Or some days? Someday, in retrospect? A few months after we started dating, Shelly and I were talking with a woman recently widowed. She and her husband had been happily married, she said, for more than fifty years. What's the secret? "We changed tires together," she said, and went on to explain they had shared the mundane and the adventures. They built a history together that she thought nourished their longevity and happiness.

Moving to Haiti together is like changing tires—times a thousand. To this point, smiles and laughter are still plentiful between us. (And yes, I'm turning down the regular, generous offers by young men in the community to help find a mistress for me. They offer out of kindness, though also, I think, to gauge what I think of Haitians in general, to see what kind of intimacy I'm willing to have with the community. But this would definitely not be the best way to prove my lack of prejudice. So I laugh and say, "Thanks. You're right, she's really pretty—but I love Shelly, and she's the only one for me.")

These are far from optimal conditions for intimacy: the walls of our room are about six feet high, only two-thirds of the way to the ceiling. And the person lying next to Shelly is hardly a sculpted Brad Pitt these days (okay, never was, but especially not now). Despite eating as much rice as possible, I'm shrinking into a fragile supermodel type, with heroin-chic, sunken cheeks and a pronounced collarbone. Not that I was bulky to begin with, at six feet two, 185 pounds, but I now weigh about 157 and am shrinking quickly. About every six days I have a serious thirty-six-hour bout of vomiting and diarrhea from a persistent case of giardia—little round amoebas that apparently like to frolic in our local water supply. Well, at least they're in my intestines and not my testicles. I've been to the hospital and am taking medicine; we'll see what happens. We use a good filter, but you can't cut off all contact with water in juices, ice, washed dishes and vegetables, and bathing, especially when you're living with a family and accepting other people's hospitality.

Maybe I could raise development money by occasionally hitting the Paris catwalks with my newly svelte figure. Or market a new diet: "Just drink this eight-ounce pouch of water straight from the

Woshdlo source! Call 1-800-SKINNY to begin the Caribbean Slimming Plan!"*

So even if I weren't ruining my chances with "Get away from me" during the afternoon and with walls not going all the way to the ceiling at night, I'm not in peak lover condition. At times I've been so weak and unsteady, Shelly has come into the little latrine enclosed by woven banana leaves and, so I don't fall over, held me as I squat over the concrete hole in the ground. There's something deeply tender (if on occasion slightly gross) about the intimate ways we're sharing life, even though our relationship has never been more tense and awkward and needs some changes.

                    ⌒

Being pushed to my limits in every way brings back Jesus' question to the rich young man. I've answered in part but still feel like I'm being asked, "What are you willing to give up?"

So you gain everything by losing everything. What does that mean in real life?

There are plenty of people peddling definitive theoretical, self-help and theological answers. It's the personal answers that are more interesting—and demanding—though. Really personal. What am I willing to give up to follow Jesus and to help others? Things that make life comfortable. The little and big lies (mostly to self and some to others) that make getting through the day easier. There's money, of course, and all it buys. There's being successful, being hip, being right, being good, being respected. There are ambitions and lust.

These days, whether living around the corner from a Burger King or living here, where the nearest bacon double cheeseburger

---

*Not FDA approved. Possible side effects include leaning against a tree in your yard, vomiting as the neighbor kids watch, then weakly stumbling back into the 110-degree bedroom where you decide to lie on the dirty carpet rather than the bed because it's only 109 degrees down there.

seems a million miles away, I think part of the answer is another pair of questions: What is in the way of my loving more? And what am I *going to do now* to starve this desire—so I can hunger for something better?

AS YOU LEAVE THE VILLAGE . . .

It's What You Might Dare Hope They'd Say (Though It Would Be Impudent to Admit as Much, and No Way You Could Say It, and It's Not Completely True, and Who Knows What It Portends)

After seven months, on our last day living with our Woshdlo family before moving out on our own, Shelly and I awake to the not unusual sound of Grandfather praying aloud at 4:00 a.m. For almost an hour he thanks *Bondye* and Jesus for his many blessings, prays for his family and for us, and sings hymns unrestrained as morning light eases in. Soon everyone is up and preparing for the goodbye party, including a steadily increasing number of village women who come to help with cutting and cooking and with the sitting around and taste-testing and talking too. The smell of the spices from the chicken (the best fried chicken I've ever had) wafts throughout the *lakou*. With my Creole now adept enough for errands, I am sent to buy paper plates and plastic cups, forks, spoons. At various times Grandfather and I cross paths on the dirt roads; he is chasing down an ice truck to arrange delivery. Shelly shreds cabbage with a pocket knife for three hours (the longer and thinner the slices, the better).

As the day progresses, the kids, who are running prep errands, get progressively more hyper. At one point an eighteen-month-old cousin is so overwhelmed by the energy and anticipation around him that he just falls to the dirt ground (he's naked) and starts rolling back and forth in laughter.

This carries me back to another dinner, in Albania—one that was part of leading me to this moment after seven months here in Haiti.

At that dinner I concentrated on the beady little fish eyes that kept staring at me. As a distraction and for revenge, and because I was hungry, I focused on technique: two precise bites—one on each side—and a few nibbles stole all the meat from each of the thin, five-inch long, silvery black fish that Vera had piled on my plate. But removing the meat just made their unblinking gaze more grotesque. Each became, on a small side plate to my left, a floating head connected by a frail, centipede-like spine to a thin tail. The spines, some healthy and white, some sickly yellow, were exposed and naked.

Vera in Albanian means "spring." She was the spunky, dark-haired matriarch of the family I'd lived with for four months in Shkodēr, Albania, where I was working with a local Albanian Protestant church to distribute food, mattresses and clothes to Kosovar refugees. She and her family lived in the two rooms downstairs; the two upstairs rooms were mine.

Vera had olive skin, an athletic body, a handsome jaw and intensity in everything she did—whether scrubbing the floor, poking fun at my strange American ways or making dinner for her family. She was about thirty years old, though like seemingly everyone else in the country, she looked more worn than her years. In the evenings, when I came home exhausted after a full day of giving out supplies, she often said, "You my brother; I your sister," before asking for English tips or laughing at my few Albanian phrases.

This was several years before Haiti and a few months after I'd started dating Shelly. I had moved into Vera's house two weeks before Milošević pulled out of Kosovo, thereby ending the nighttime rumble of NATO planes flying overhead toward Serbia. The refugees we'd been assisting stayed in town for a few months after the war was over but had recently returned to their scorched homes. Tomorrow morning I was leaving Albania to work in Pejë, Kosovo.

I knew the night's agenda because Vera had told my Albanian friends, who in turn told me. The whole evening was to be a carefully calculated petition. I knew it wouldn't be fun, but it seemed like the right thing to do. I'd paid rent, but still Vera and her family had been kind and generous with me, though they had little. The least I could do was listen.

After dismounting a rusty bike, I walked with a hint of martyr's swagger toward the door with my Albanian friend who would translate. (For the last few nights before leaving, I was sleeping at the church where I'd been working.) I was greeted with a hug from Vera's seven-year-old boy, a fragile leaf who liked math, had the sunken raccoon eyes of an addict and was destined for a shaky life in this machismo-drenched Balkan culture. I threw the four-year-old girl, a cute little terror, into the air, eliciting squeals of joy. Vera's husband, with whom I'd shared an occasional beer and watched the European Cup (he cheered for Germany) on the constantly blaring television, was at work. Then I greeted Vera. More subdued than I'd ever seen her, she said hi but kept her eyes toward the floor. The kids were banished to the bedroom as the three of us—Vera, my Albanian friend and me—went into the family's other room. This was the best I'd seen the kids behave without first being stung by the switch Vera had broken off a tree outside.

The aroma of a feast welcomed us. The table was loaded with fresh bread; a steak of sweetly cooked fish; another plate piled high with the small, silvery black fish; tomatoes, cucumbers, onions; beer and *raki,* the local grape brandy as volatile as the region's history. A hodgepodge of stuffed animals and knickknacks decorated the room.

Soon after sitting down to dinner, Vera, looking at the table, told me she had a large lump behind her left ear. It was cancerous, she feared. I think I touched it, though I can't remember clearly; I know she asked me to. The doctors had told her there was nothing they could do, that her only hope was the West, that only America could save her now.

I was wealth, she was poverty. With that clear, Vera talked with my friend in Albanian and left me, in her mind at least, to decide whether she lived or died, whether the squealing delight of her little girl, who liked singing and dancing to Spice Girls videos, would become the searing loss of a motherless child.

I ate more of the small fish. They kept staring at me.

As the dinner continued, Vera kept topping off my glass of *raki* every time I took a sip. I hadn't received translation for some time, except for the occasional "I am glad you are not sick. I would do everything for you." As a finale, she pleaded, begged, for my help. I was impotent, frustrated, depleted, sad. I told her about a Canadian doctor who could look at her next time he was in town.

It was late and time to leave. The night had closed in like a casket. For months my nights had been locked up in this little house. Sunsets tinged with oranges and purples were also tainted by fear and loneliness in this isolated and violent city. Everyone abandoned the streets at dusk because they became unsafe. Tonight my friend and I would ride our bikes with silent urgency to the church, where we would sleep.

My routine for the last four months had been to come back to Vera's at sunset, play for a little while with the kids, then go upstairs, lock the door, read for a few minutes and fall asleep. Two or three times, very late, after I had been asleep for some time, I awoke suddenly to what I thought was the sound of soft knocking on my door. Flooded with the adrenaline of waking suddenly, I tried to conjure an image behind the darkened door. In my jolted state, I wondered if I had really heard anything. The darkness was charged with fear and mystery. I wondered if it was my frazzled imagination or if it was Vera, if she had come up the stairs for comfort, to lie in my bed while her husband worked the night shift and the kids slept downstairs.

I never answered that soft—or imaginary—knock. But at this final dinner I still felt like the guilty lover who had enjoyed the affair and now wanted to fade into the night without cost, without words of accusation, without having to look at each other one last time. It was good while it lasted, I thought, so let's leave it at that. Vera wanted more; she wouldn't let me off that easy. She was speaking words about our relationship that were true but that were better left unsaid, unspoken words that had made the playful tryst with her family possible. Now that these words were articulated, we couldn't look each other in the eyes. Now we left each other empty and broken, angry and jealous.

As I mounted my bike and we said goodbye, Vera became cheery again. At the time I thought it was a weak final effort either to manipulate or gloss over her manipulation, but in retrospect I know it was also to regain some dignity before I left. Now I was the one brooding, kicking the gravel as I ached for the physical sensation of pushing my pedals and accelerating into the night. By not looking at her, I tried to avoid her exposed desperation, avoid the demanding stories of Jesus, avoid the eyes of those fish that got up off their plates, their centipede spines wiggling back and forth to swim after me as I biked away, that have been writhing after me ever since.

After moving back to Princeton, I had scarce contact with my friends in Albania—people with whom I had shared meals, laughed, played chess and worked. I smile remembering when I turned down Vera's offer, in front of the kids, to show me the family Kalashnikov. I wonder about Vera, her family, the lump behind her left ear. I should have done more, but I was empty, with nothing left to give. Instead of being one small battle I could try to help win, she represented an overwhelming reality that I couldn't take on. I see Vera in my memory, but not her eyes. Shame and guilt make remembrance blurry, protect their patron.

The fish followed me back to Princeton and were no doubt part of chasing me to Haiti. A standard response to visiting a poor country is sympathy and a new perspective that leads people to say things like, "It just makes you so thankful for what we have, makes you appreciate the country we live in." But it had the opposite effect on me: I found it almost impossible to be thankful because I felt haunted by the situation of others. I needed to try again to chase after the vision of Amos, one of those raging prophets in Scripture.

Israel was in a prosperous time, but the bounty was hoarded by the powerful few who were exploiting the poor. This clashed with God's vision, which is made vividly—and violently—clear throughout Amos's judgment. Speaking of the rich he says, "For I know how many are your transgressions, / and how great are your sins— / you who afflict the righteous, who take a bribe, / and push aside the needy in the gate" (5:12). (It's not the same gate as in Jesus' story about Lazarus and the poor man, but the parallels are there.)

God rejects and despises worship and faith that are not linked to justice. The implications are both personal and for all of society. The consequences for those who "trample on the needy, / and bring to ruin the poor of the land" (8:4) are bleak: "On that day, says the Lord GOD, / I will make the sun go down at noon, / and darken the earth in broad daylight. / I will turn your feasts into mourning, / and all your songs into lamentation; / . . . I will make it like the mourning for an only son, / and the end of it like a bitter day" (8:9-10).

But also, thankfully, we're reminded that while there's a lot of righteous anger here, ultimately it's about love and redemption, hope and even joy. At the end of the book, Amos offers God's ethereal vision of harmony that seems to say no one will know *true happiness* until everyone knows happiness, until everyone shares in the bounty as "the mountains shall drip sweet wine, / and all the hills shall flow with it" (9:13).

⌒

Now, back in Woshdlo, at the dinner celebrating our seven months together and their sending us off to work in Port-au-Prince, I feel like I've been able to really start looking into people's eyes. Guests start arriving in late afternoon. It is fun chaos of grabbing bites to eat and handing out plates of food. About a hundred guests each receive a plate full of a few deep-fried plantains, *pikliz* (tangy cabbage salad), beet salad, a few pieces of lettuce, a piece or two of chicken, rice and beans, as well as a Coke, Sprite or beer. Saying hi, saying bye. All around the *lakou*, people eat, drink, talk and laugh. Shelly and I make small thank-you speeches, as do some family members and a few other guests. The local postmaster takes his chance as an honored guest to pitch the services available through the improving post office, which will hopefully soon acquire a motor scooter so he can make deliveries. Before and after the speeches, the small radio is blaring. The night eventually dwindles to just family and a few neighbors dancing in the dark.

During the brief party speeches, the son-in-law, the one who had entertained at the welcome party with the joke about the phone call from hell to Haiti, had quoted from Martin Luther King Jr.'s "I Have a Dream," in a good preacher's cadence and heavily accented English: "I have a dream that one day sons of former slaves and sons of former slave owners will be able to sit down together at a table of brotherhood. . . . Free at last, free at last; thank God Almighty, we are free at last." Then he added in Creole, "I think Martin Luther King would be smiling if he saw us now and how we have lived with each other for the past seven months."

Shelly and I are, of course, profoundly encouraged by his words.

Though actually no, neither they nor we are yet "free at last." Yes, thank God the chains of slavery have been shattered, but poverty and politics (as well as wealth and too much power) still keep a strangling grip. He knows this too, of course. But he was saying it was remarkable that white middle-class Americans and poor black Haitians could live like family, even temporarily. Together we sat at the table, bathed in the yard, hand-washed laundry and shucked beans, worked a little in the garden, listened to Grandmother's stories, walked to market with the sisters, did homework with the grandkids, cared for and helped and learned from one another (though they certainly helped us far more than we helped them). Tomorrow Shelly and I move out on our own to discover, work and live in simmering Port-au-Prince.

UNDER THE WARDROBE

A rat scurries into the room, runs past my bare right foot and disappears under a wardrobe about a yard from the place on the floor where I will sleep tonight. I'd earlier heard the little beast knocking about a few pots and pans in the dining/living room. With bubonic plague–like efficiency, it killed my ability to focus. So now I scratch out this sentence staccato style—glancing down . . . every few seconds . . . looking . . . for signs . . . of the rat . . . or its compatriots. Hiding under the darkest corner of the rough-hewn wooden wardrobe to my right (I have no evidence of this, except my charged imagination) is a bustling, multigenerational nest of decrepit, disease-ridden rats; vigorous, attack rats; and red-eyed baby rats, naked and pink and blind and grappling all over one another.

Pause, look down, scan around. No sign of it. But my senses are on blazing red alert. A few months ago a colleague here in Haiti recounted her story of being awakened by a rat blowing on her ("a little puff of air"). Her sudden waking scared the rat away. The explanation was that this is a common rat method of testing whether its prey is dead or alive before biting in. Whether or why this would be true, I don't know, but do you doubt I will feel a thousand little puffs of foul rat breath—every few seconds, all over my body—when I lie down to sleep?

After leaving Woshdlo, this is our second night here on a mountainside in the village of Mòn Zaboka, just above Port-au-Prince. It's close to the office where we'll begin working full time with Beyond Borders. We're staying in the home of another Haitian family—Jean Louis, Jezina and their three children. We'll stay for just two weeks, until our house-sitting begins for colleagues who live nearby.

Tonight is not the first time rats have thieved my sleep since moving to Haiti. In Woshdlo, little pellets were appearing regularly on our room's carpet floor. An occasional suspicious noise. One night a suspect shadow—too large for a mouse, too small for a cat—creeping across an overhead beam. Then a grapefruit rind that was mysteriously transported during the night from the neighboring room to the middle of our floor—again, a few feet from our bed. In the room we just left behind in Woshdlo, our double bed was raised and enclosed in a mosquito net. Of course Mr. Rat could have chewed through the net in two seconds, but it felt like significant (if only psychological) armor. At least to my conscious mind. My subconscious wasn't so impressed—and as a precaution against malaria I was taking chloroquine, which can trigger disturbing dreams. Over several months, I had six or seven vivid nightmares in which I was under attack by an unidentifiable rat-sized animal in my bed. The first time, when Shelly tried to comfort me—reaching over to wake me from my grunting and thrashing—I thought her touch was the attacking animal, so I struck at her then recoiled into a ball. In subsequent cases, she just said my name and, "It's okay . . . it's just a dream . . . you're okay."

The worst of the nightmares sent me yelling and scrambling out from under the carefully secured mosquito net. I awoke standing naked in the middle of the room, with my heart beating like a hysterical Vodou drum and with Shelly saying in Creole to the son-in-law, whom I'd awakened and who was out of his bed and ready to burst through the door that connected our rooms to see if he could help with whatever horrible emergency was underway, "*Non, non, tout bagay anfòm. Se sèlman yon rèv. Tout bagay anfòm.*" "No, no, it's okay. It was just a dream. Everything's okay." Shelly's words were incomprehensible to me as I stood there, naked, stunned, panting—looking as through gauze at the room in dim lamplight, seeing Shelly under the collapsed mosquito net, wondering what was happening, knowing my fear was still elusive, prowling, on the loose.

Though I'm squeamish about rats (who isn't?), the terror of these dreams wasn't solely rats. A rat was just a convenient incarnation of other nearby fears. How safe are we in this land with tremendous need and a sometimes volatile and bloody history, both ancient and recent? Am I doing more harm than good? Wait, does that scratching along the tin roof followed by the dead-weight slithering of a tail signal the arrival of reinforcements? Did my parents lie to my siblings and me twenty years ago when they told us they were setting *mouse*traps in our rented cottage at Yellowstone National Park? Is hope reasonable or only escapist fantasy to avoid cruel, indifferent reality? Are the ideals that propelled me to Haiti just privileged naivete and presumption? These fears are ultimately about not being in control; stressful conditions just exacerbate them. But now a rat—before, just a dream symbol of my anxieties—has appeared in the flesh to trigger twitching muscles and prickly skin, while under the surface, the various fears metastasize, gnawing at my insides, taking over my mind and body like a cancerous power.

For the first time I notice how closely a shoelace resembles a rat's tail. My tennis shoe keeps grabbing my jittery eye's attention as the muted kerosene lamp bleeds faint but ominous shadows around the room. And did I just hear a claw scratching along the cement behind me? Spin, look—not there.

When the rat first invaded, I leapt back out of my chair, squealed like a schoolgirl and scared my sleeping wife. Shelly drowsily assured me it would be highly effective to put a single, lit candle on the floor behind my chair, between the wardrobe and this mat on the floor—and quickly returned into deep sleep. But before declaring her a paragon of courage, realize that she's on a small metal-frame cot, a good twenty-four inches off the ground. There was only one bed, and I wanted Shelly to have it. I got the floor/the feeding area. I'm sitting at a small table covered by a large white doily with a kerosene lamp on it. In front of me, to my right, is the doorway to the rest of the house. There's no door, only a see-through, frilly pink curtain that couldn't keep a hamster out. The wardrobe/rat bunker extends back on my right. The lone candle sits on the floor behind me. The mattress extends back on the floor to my left, with Shelly on the cot to its left and flush to the wall. At the foot of my mattress is an open bucket of urine, because at night here you don't go to the outhouse, you pee in a bucket. The floor is concrete, as are the dirty white walls; the roof is corrugated tin. Little beetle/cockroach hybrids are playing chase across my paper and the table. There. Focusing briefly on what is visible by the faint light, rather than on what is invisible in the shadows, is therapeutic.

I remember another rat encounter years ago—and it's turning into a metaphor about avoiding disagreeable truth. When working in Albania, during a break one afternoon, a teenage Albanian friend, Ares, and I were playing chess on the first floor of the small church, which had been transformed into a storage area where we packed goods in big black garbage bags before distributing them to refugees the next day. As we shuffled our pawns, rooks and bishops, we heard rustling in the bags. We ignored it. Then more vigorous movement. We picked up a roll of tape and threw it at the noise in the pile of black bags. Two cats fled the scene and out of the church. Problem solved, back to chess. Advance a knight to a center square, then more rustling from the same spot. Another cat? Let's investigate. We kick at the bags. Find the moving one. A mischievous feline must have actually gotten inside a bag. We kick at it more. It moves but makes no noise and doesn't escape the bag. Curious. Now we look for a tool. The best we can do is an aerosol can of bathroom cleaner. Divvying up tasks, I pick up and hold the bag as Ares prods the creature in an attempt to identify it. It moves around, but no noise. Then Ares's demeanor darkens and he unleashes—hitting and smashing and hitting. Eventually the bag stops moving. We carry it out to the courtyard and I dump out the contents. Amidst the raining pitter-patter of loose sugar and the soft snowfall of flour comes the rude tumble of a dirty, gray, mammoth rat, limp and oozing red spots of blood from its bashed-in brain.

Besides at this moment deriving pleasure by recalling that particular rat's demise and besides hoping the nearby hiding rat is not a Haitian relative of that deceased Albanian rat, here to exact familial revenge, maybe that incident—at least at this late hour—speaks of how we avoid, whether consciously or not, ugly truth until it just can't be ignored anymore. I like to consider myself someone who chooses (when it's within my capability) to know the truth, even if unsettling. But last night I heard suspicious noises whose cause, though unconfirmed, wasn't actually that mysterious . . . and I slept. Tonight I've confirmed the cause with my own eyes . . . and I'm jumpy, insomniac.

Maybe tomorrow I'll go down the mountain to an Internet café in Port-au-Prince for research on rats. Look up how they spread disease. Find an estimate of the toll they've collected in human death. Look up what positive contribution they (and while I'm at it, mosquitoes) could possibly be making to our planet. Why, Creator, why? Finally, I'll Google nonprofits dedicated to working for the extinction of rats—and make a sizable though ultimately useless credit-card contribution.

Meanwhile, a possibly malarial (okay, I don't know if there's malaria in this region) mosquito keeps circle-buzzing my ear. Bring on malaria; Haiti has a mild form, anyway. Sign me up for this unholy arrangement: I'll take malaria; you provide rat protection.

More seriously, should I follow my brain where it scurries now? What else to do? What more appropriate subjects than sex or God in the early a.m. hours? Shelly is sleeping soundly in her cot twenty-four inches off the ground, which leaves God.

So this seems to be turning into a prayer, though it might be a little disingenuous when I'm poised to instantly bolt from my chair and scream "Ah! Ahhh! *EEEEkkk!*" if that rat scampers out from under there and toward me. Can you pray with one eye half open, nervously scanning for shadow-vermin? I again need to turn away from self and toward God (and others), that liberating movement of prayer. Because really, at some time during these hours I should confess that millions and millions of poor and hungry and imprisoned people, in Haiti and elsewhere, have much more serious nightly rat problems than do I. As do their children. I need only think of the gorgeous little cross-eyed, six-year-old girl sleeping on a floor mat just like mine in a room across the hall. (Jean Louis's family can't afford the necessary ophthalmologic care.) I've moved to Haiti to live with, work alongside and learn from those who are much more economically poor than I. But now I'm obsessed about *my* rat, not theirs. I want to acknowledge *their* rats, too, which are teeming and relentless and worse: "God, protect us tonight from evil—especially, though not only, from rats. And please, protect us *all*. Amen."

Early a.m., rats, truth, prayer, evil: it seems justifiable to take a quick stab at something that, like rodents and cockroaches, usually stays out of sight, out of mind, during the busy daylight but sneaks out during the lonely darkness. Why did God send Jesus to be crucified rather than sending Jesus to crucify rats (by which I mean both the figurative *rats* that are the power of evil around us and in us, to which we're so frightfully susceptible and so excruciatingly exposed, as well as literal *rats*)? I know the theological theories, but bloody and squealing rats nailed to those rough crossbeams—where his hands were, his feet—on Golgotha . . . now that would have rippled out indisputable reason to rejoice and praise through the millennia. God and all of us know we could do with an omnipotent pest and rodent exterminator down here. And Jesus does sort of appear this way in Scripture, but not till his still-awaited, second time coming. It's a fearful thing at this hour, the idea of the divine return for a final pest control (that is, for judgment and redemption)—because I imagine the cleansing will be painful, no matter who we are, since each of us is infested to some extent. But in all my naked, late-night honesty, it's about the only thing that gives me real hope—hope that's big enough for evil that's so big, so complicated, so everywhere, so unreachably hidden under our wardrobes and so deep in our hearts.

The more I think about it, the more this turn in the meditation seems appropriate. God fits in this rat narrative, since the grand "Why am I here?" is now running through my mind again and again—even if it's less in the abstractly theological sense, more in the petty, specific sense of this room, this night, next to this wardrobe. So here it goes again, with fear and sleeplessness and loneliness stripping away the self-protection and the irony and the cynicism, reaching for an outrageous hope. I pray, in the most literal and apocalyptic sense, not as a cheap plea to escape a nearby rat tonight: *Come, Lord Jesus, come. And please, this time finish the job.*

Thirty minutes later. On that prayerful note, I had laid down my pen and then laid myself down to sleep on the floor, secretly hoping that God would be so impressed with my piety that I'd miraculously float into safe slumber. *Dear Almighty, remember protecting Daniel in that den of ravenous lions? Much smaller request, this: just one rat that has already been snacking in the kitchen.* But for half an hour I kept falling toward sleep . . . then realizing what an insane, defenseless position that would leave me in . . . so jerking back wide awake. Exhausted. Now this is surely less about truth or evil or God, more about clawing my way toward morning light, scratching toward the rat's bedtime, combating against perilous sleep. Too vulnerable. Angry at myself. I can almost feel the rat puffing noxious fumes on me before digging its two oversize front teeth into my flesh, or scrambling over my bare upper arm and then disappearing back under the wardrobe to watch me, mock me, hunt me again.

Dawn still seems forever away, but I'm drained of strength. And what else lurks under there?

CATS

I've never liked cats. My earliest childhood memory of them involves sitting on a family friend's porch and petting kittens as my eyes turned into fiery, swollen itch-balls and my lungs strained to wheeze in each new breath. Since that day, I've always held cats (a.k.a., marauding dander factories) in disdain, though I would admit kittens are mildly cute—from an uncompromised distance.

Until last week. The night after my sleepless rat visit, I joined Shelly on her tiny, unstable, severely concave, smaller-than-a-twin-bed cot where we then spent two weeks of long, fitful nights tangling and untangling our limbs.

That was then. Now I sleep anxiety-free because cute little, precious little, brave little Mitsu prowls the two-room concrete house where we've since moved.

What can I say about Mitsu? She's a three-month-old kitten. She's special enough to merit her own name rather than the generic *Mimi* given to most Haitian cats. We're two weeks into a sixteen-week house-sitting assignment for our friends and colleagues John and Merline. We're plotting already to take Mitsu with us when we move. She's a modern-art rendition of a miniaturized tiger, with black and orange splotches around her body, with one ear tipped black and the other tipped orange, with white boots and white painting down the bridge of her nose to her whiskers and on down to her chest and tummy.

Oh, and did I say *she?* She's actually a *he.* Apparently due to gender discrimination, his cuteness has compelled us, against the facts, to regularly call *him* a *her.*

But while the misplaced personal pronoun is about cuteness, the story of reversal isn't. Like I said, kittens always remained mildly cute to me, even after that day on a friend's porch when cats came to mean strained breathing and swollen eyes. So it's not just rediscovering kitty cuteness that has me picking up Mitsu when I first awaken each morning and again when I come home at the end of the day, holding him and baby-talking to him in English/Creole gibberish. Cuteness alone doesn't propel me to joyfully serve him each day by digging through his kitty litter to extract granule-coated turds. No, this reversal is about usefulness.

Now, cat-loving purists might discount my love because it's based on utility. I disagree. My commitment is based neither on infatuation nor aesthetic inclination nor mere magnetic (animal) attraction toward cats rather than, say, dogs. This connection to my little Mitsu-pitsu results from a new dependence on the earth's processes, such as rainwater and local harvests and natural solutions to natural problems. That the relationship was born of a primitive exchange—the kitten needs food and water, we need rat protection—doesn't, for me, taint it at all. This exchange is the realistic soil in which cuddling and lovey-dovey baby-talk have blossomed.

Proof that this path to love is even purer than standard domestic housecat affection can be found in the costs of the relationship—namely, the wheezing of allergies and the risk of love. First, the allergies. I now have a constant, slight wheeze. Twice I've barely slept for an entire night because my embattled lungs demanded my body's full, unsleeping effort to breathe. Daily doses of nasal spray and allergy syrup usually take the edge off.

Second, a few days ago Shelly and I trampled through the thickly wooded area behind our house, risking a fall every few feet on the mountainside's steep incline, as we cried out, "Mitsuuuuuu! Mitsuuuu! *Ki kote ou ye? Vini, Mitsuu!* Where are you? Come here, Mitsuuu!" (As a dual-citizen pet of an American husband and Haitian wife, we're not sure whether he prefers English or Creole, or if he's fully bilingual.) The three ornery dogs we're also house-sitting had chased Mitsu far into the woods. I was genuinely worried. How will he survive out there in the wild? How will he find his way back?

"She's an animal," said Shelly. "They know how to do those things." I wasn't so sure; he's so precious and vulnerable (though also—I can see it in his eyes—a vicious slayer of rats). But sure enough, a couple of hours later when rain started to fall, he returned.

Quickly, have I mentioned the intensity of Mitsu's sideways leaps, with arched back like a deranged spider, as he elaborately hunts . . . a leaf? How he sits like aristocracy, spine erect with black and orange tail wrapped elegantly around his immaculate white boots? How he tilts his head slightly to the side as I call him, not moving at all, keeping all his dignity as I lose mine with increasingly desperate beckoning? How he ducks into my hand, shaping his spine to the movement of my caress? How his little sandpaper tongue licks peanut butter off my fingertip?

Is it obvious that Shelly and I don't yet have children? Two and a half years into marriage, we've become one of those couples that treats their pets as such. Common wisdom has pet rearing as a useful precursor to child rearing—a trial run on sharing responsibility, deciding punishment and so on. We're softies, sticking only (and halfheartedly) to the rule of Mitsu's not being allowed on the bed or tables. We hand-feed him avocados. Shelly disciplines with humorously stern rebukes in Creole; I tend for soft smacks on the behind. Does this foretell dissension about corporal punishment for our children? Maybe, since Shelly mocks me by saying, "Go ahead, just hit her again, why don't you?"

A few mornings ago, as demonstration of our ineffectiveness with the No Sleeping nor Ever Coming Up on Our Bed rule, Shelly awoke with little Mitsu curled up in the nape of her neck. She then tenderly informed me, "When I get old, after you die, I'm going to get four or five cats and let them sleep with me." There are, of course, two disturbing aspects of this statement. First, there's the reminder of my mortality. Second, and more disturbing at the moment, there's the concern that Shelly will one day become a "cat lady."

I tried to explain that one cute kitten curled up in your bed *now* is entirely different from the inevitable downward spiral of having four or five cats as an octogenarian with diminished cleaning capability, followed by unseen litters of innumerable kittens under the recesses of the increasingly hair-covered sofa, which means more cats, and it all just goes so horribly wrong and ends up as a freak obituary in the local newspaper after Shelly follows me into death and is then found in her unkept cat-infested apartment. To retrieve her body, the EMTs have to wade through a living room waist-deep in kittens, cats, fur, hairballs, kitty litter and cat food and past the shredded blinds and wood furniture carved into monstrosities by sharpening claws.

Unconvinced, Shelly says, "Well, I'll be lonely, and they're warm and cuddly. I want to have four or five cats, and you won't be able to do anything about it."

So, yes, I still have my cat limits. But now Mitsu is curled up on my lap as I sit here in dim lamplight on a Haitian mountainside in a tiny concrete-block house. Mitsu's purr is rumbling like a smooth-running little motor: *RRRrrrrrrrrrRRRrrrrrrrrrRRRrrrr.* It's sweet and funny—such tangible, vibrating contentedness. I had never before been close enough—or shared a moment special enough—to know what it felt like when cats purred.

I need Mitsu, and he needs me. I don't know what any of this means for my future relationship with cats—especially if there comes a time and place where I no longer need rat protection. But right now, for a few minutes, Mitsu and I are content to be grateful and to briefly not worry about the past or the future.

It's a momentary retreat on this island that suffers too much sadness. The answers to the question "What do I live for?" press in so urgently on most days that I feel the insistent demands pushing away the answer. *Live for love,* Jesus answered. *Love God. Love your neighbor.*

Let love guide each decision, whether small or life-changing, whether it impacts a neighbor or a stranger on the other side of the world or the spouse sleeping so close. Let love guide real-estate choices, vocation, neighborly relations, use of water and food. Even, Saint Francis would say, how I treat my cat (though I don't care what he would say about rats).

Saint Paul famously wrote in 1 Corinthians 13 that love never fails. Maybe God's doesn't, but the rest of ours does with frequency that would be comic if not so tragic. Still, we can keep testing how far love will carry us, and in the testing we uncover new goodness and joy.

4

Choosing One's Neighbors

BUILDING A HOME (PART I)

Houses, fields and vineyards will again be bought in this land.

JEREMIAH 32:15

Fire ants are biting at our ankles as Shelly and I scout out the small, overgrown plot of land in Mòn Zaboka with Jean Louis. It's August 2003, eight months after arriving in Haiti. Slipping, sliding, almost rolling ankles on avocado pits, we make our way through the brush, past sour orange, avocado and mango trees to look at this clearing as a place to potentially build a house. The land once belonged to a long-dead uncle of Jean Louis but was sold to our friends John and Merline. There it is: a beautiful little flat spot nestled into the mountainside, surrounded by an abundance of green leaves. (Though even lushness is a melancholy reminder of how this country has been stripped of so much natural, tropical splendor.) A field of drying cornhusks, recently harvested, ascends the hill above. To the side and down into a small valley extends a sloping garden of small, spindly Congo bean trees.

Shelly and I have started working full time at the Beyond Borders office. The next four months of house-sitting are set, but we have to start figuring out where to live, some place sustainable and relatively close to the office, when they return. Jean Louis pauses and says, "Here it is. Here's where Lafrique used to live."

Jean Louis has an infectious laugh that is easily triggered, whether by humor or exasperation. Like so many, he has to scramble to get by. In addition to serving as the director of a local Catholic church that has a small elementary school, Jean Louis sells phone cards, works on local construction projects, finds other odd jobs and hangs out at a barbershop in between. He wears pressed slacks, leather sandals and Cuban smoking shirts (often with a few little holes and stains from wear) that are *de rigueur* for Haitian pastors and priests. His family history extends far back in this area, but Jean Louis says little about his uncle Lafrique. It's evident only that he's been dead long enough that the stone walls of his house have mostly crumbled. What remains is a three-foot-high outline overgrown by bushes and long grass. His tiny abode couldn't have housed much more than a bed.

I feel a sense of intruding as we step over one of the crumbling walls into the old house. Looking back down the mountain through the trees, I glimpse slices of Port-au-Prince, a hot, bustling, explosive city that is brewing a political crisis stemming back, in part, to President Jean-Bertrand Aristide's role in flawed legislative elections more than three years ago in May 2000. The city is also heroic with its 2.5 million people fighting to make life work. (Quick geographical note: Port-au-Prince's downtown is near sea level, and the city climbs up the surrounding mountainsides. As it gets higher, Port-au-Prince merges into Pétionville. In some ways they're indistinguishable, but significant differences exist too. Pétionville is where many of the tiny upper class live and shop and is farther from the most densely populated, poorest slums in the heart of Port-au-Prince. The little mountain village of Mòn Zaboka is just on the edge of Pétionville. For simplicity, I mostly speak of both cities as Port-au-Prince.) Up here at the moment, politics and city life seem far away, and Jean Louis is preaching about how quickly and easily a simple two-roomed house could materialize on this plot, which would only require chopping down three adolescent avocado trees to clear space.

I feel a tug of solidarity. I would welcome humbly trying to stake a claim here, making an effort toward something long-term. Then I catch Shelly's eye and realize I'm intoxicated by ideals and possibilities. With brief clarity I wonder if I'm just a fool following a (self- and others-) destructive path like that imagined in Paul Theroux's *Mosquito Coast*. When the fire ants bite, the sharp sting doesn't take effect for five or ten seconds; by the time you smack at them, they're already attacking farther up your leg.

Shelly and I walk back around the potential site several times over the next few weeks and have many conversations with Jean Louis, with John and Merline, with each other. At first we just toy with the idea. It would be ridiculous to build a house in an unstable country where we still aren't fully fluent in the language or culture. Neither of us knows anything about construction in any country. We can't afford much financial risk. But . . . we could easily work out a land deal with John and Merline, and the project would be convenient to oversee as we house-sit until December at their two-room, tin-roofed house just one hundred feet from the site. We don't want to move to yet another community at the end of the year. The commute to our office would be a doable fifty-minute hike and public transportation ride. We would provide construction jobs in a nation where only a third of the people are formally employed, the rest having to scratch out a living by farming their fields, engaging in small commerce such as selling used shoes on the street, or picking up day labor. Also standing boldly in the plus column: we can't find a better option.

We determine the maximum we could spend on a house would be three thousand dollars (about a year-and-a-half's rent for a simple place in the city). We check numbers with Jean Louis. He says we could build what we wanted for twenty-five hundred dollars. We tell him that's perfect, that's our maximum. He assures us it could be finished by early December. We double-check this price and timeline with others who have building experience here. In one of these conversations with Jean Louis, I already sully this ideal-driven project by telling him an unpremeditated lie: that to build we would need a salary advance. Not true. I wanted to be sure he understood our finances were tight, since the assumption is often that Americans have unlimited resources. Though three thousand dollars is a pretty good deal for a house, we had earned nothing in the past seven months, and now we each made eight hundred dollars per month. Our salaries were geared toward middle-class Haitian standards rather than the higher level of foreign aid workers and even missionaries. Yet I still found myself slipping in a lie because I'm embarrassed by the comparative wealth at our disposal. We're also embarrassed to tell our family back in Woshdlo that we're building our own two-room house for just the two of us, when they still sleep three-plus people per room, with at least two people per twin-size bed.

When Jean Louis drops by on the morning of September 22, with some reluctance and a little excitement (more from me than Shelly), we say, *"Ann ale."* "Let's do it."

⌀

The next morning a few workers gather to assess the first stage. They say a wheelbarrow is needed before they can start clearing the land. The leader of the four-man land-clearing team is Maxime, previously known to us as the Coca-Cola vendor a ten-minute walk down the winding, loose-rock road toward the city. He has a big smile with a cavernous gap between his upper front teeth and hair sprouting its disorderly way toward an afro. Jean Louis says he'll get a wheelbarrow this afternoon so they can begin tomorrow morning.

As we walk back down the path, Jean Louis asks, "You don't want to build a five-thousand-dollar house, right? Just a house for two or three thousand?"

"Exactly! Two thousand five hundred dollars, maximum," we respond too emphatically. Tomorrow morning they'll start clearing the land. Shelly and I are a bit nervous; we will have so little control over this thing. Improvise. Learn. Don't regret.

I've only had two jobs that required physical labor. On graduating from high school, I was an assistant tile layer in West Palm

Beach, where the other workers called me "college boy" since that's where I was headed at the end of the summer. Then one summer during graduate school I mowed lawns in Toronto (no "grad boy" taunts, though). Also, I'm regularly teased in my family because—not counting running, shooting a basketball, hitting a racquetball, etc.—I'm unskilled at physical work of any value, like fixing a car or a basic plumbing problem, cooking or hanging a picture. Yet I secretly envision days spent working side by side with my neighbors on this mountainside, sweat beading on our brows. Despite everything I've already learned about the complexities of life and relationships here, I imagine skin color and income levels and education and nationality melting into one under the hot sun as we—neighbors and fellow workers—labor toward a most basic need of our shared humanity: shelter.

When I hear their boisterous voices this morning at 6:00 a.m., I roll over deeper into the pillow to summon energy for the Big Start. The noises blur into dreams. I reawake at 8:00 a.m. to silence and quickly walk down to the lot. The overgrown remains of Lafrique's old house are razed. Only a pile of sand remains, next to a four-foot-high pile of rocks. Brush and overgrowth have been pulled away to reveal a twenty-foot-high sloping rock cliff. Later that afternoon Jean Louis says the cliff must be cut back to make room. Shelly has agreed to move forward but has also made it clear that this is my gig. Should I back out before we launch in tomorrow?

The next day Shelly is crammed in the back of a tap-tap in the city when she sees Jean Louis leaving a stationery shop. He smiles and waves. Blueprint rolls are tucked under his arm.

A few days after my initial disappointing oversleep, three guys arrive at 7:15 a.m. I hurry outside to pursue sweaty ideals. Jean Louis is there. One man is swinging a hoe, taking out chunks of rock and earth from the sloping cliff and sweating through his faded lavender "Cowboy Cooking" T-shirt from a South Carolina restaurant. Jean Louis calls three hundred feet across the trees and gardens to Maxime, *"Vin pal ou!"* "Come talk with me!"

Yesterday at dusk Maxime came by with Jean Louis to store the new, shiny green wheelbarrow on our porch. The first moment Jean Louis turned his back, Maxime whispered to me to me that he didn't yet have enough money to send his child to school, which had started two weeks ago. I commiserated and asked more questions but offered no money. I don't think early handouts would be a good foundation for our relationship.

This morning Maxime appears from across the ravine with bare feet and a big smile. After a quick exchange, Jean Louis leaves. Then Maxime and I walk down the path to get the wheelbarrow. As he pushes the wheelbarrow back up the path, I say, "Okay, I'll come see you guys later." He responds, "And what will you bring for us when you come?"

The tropical air is warm, but the question ices my blood. I've become used to being asked for things daily, since my skin proclaims affluence. But according to an anthropological study of Haitian work groups I read a month ago (*When the Hands Are Many* by Jennie Smith), my response to Maxime at the launch of our construction project was crucial.

Rural work teams often compose songs as they labor—either to celebrate the generosity or publicize the stinginess of their employer. An example in Smith's book is this one by a work party (*konbit*) that finds their patron too stingy. I could almost hear the song echoing on the mountainside:

Down!
I say, *messieurs,*
I went to that *konbit*
I did not eat.
I went, but I found no drink

To drink.
Enough! Up!
I say, *messieurs,*
I went to that *konbit*
I found no food to eat.

Since pay rates are quite standardized, the employer is expected
to give *ankourajman,* "encouragements," to the workers—extras
like morning coffee, a midday meal of rice and beans, an occasional
shot of rum—aiming to negotiate that fine line of lubricating the
efforts and evoking good cheer without spending too much or getting the men too buzzed to work. Laborers, who need the work to
feed their families each day, have little negotiating power but lever-
age their ability to publicly shame or praise their employer.

As I head down to our office in Port-au-Prince, I stop to buy a
three-dollar bottle of three-star Barbancourt rum, though I'm not
yet sure what to do with it. I have no idea how this thing is supposed to go, but I am motivated to keep our names from melodic
disparagement in our new community. (Not that work-group
songs are always motivated by compensation issues. Bawdy humor and rumor, both of which have already been in ample supply
on the work site, also provide lyrical inspiration.)

In a new culture and language, even the simplest undertakings
can take great effort. On my way back up the mountain in the afternoon, my stomach churns like before a first date or job interview.

Arriving back at the site, my anxiety about culture, communi-
cation and customs proves unnecessary: a warm welcome awaits a
man with a full bottle of liquor and glasses in his hands. We sit in
the shade on jagged, bowling-ball-sized rocks cut out of the clearing. I learn that Maxime, his wife and their kid rent their house.
They don't have land and can't yet afford to build after living in the
area for six years. Maxime's wife, Bernadette, is with us, but he
only lets her drink half her portion, because, "I don't want her to

fall asleep and not make me dinner!" he says.

As we sip, another worker teaches me the Haitian proverb *"Chen grangou pa jwe."* "A hungry dog won't play." As he explained it, the message was this: you're doing the right thing, because it's best to keep your workers happy . . . and thus working hard.

A couple of days later, five days into the work, Jean Louis's estimate has risen to twenty-seven hundred dollars. And we're informed the new price does not include four hundred dollars for clearing the land. I'm upset—not because of the money but because it ratchets up the tension between Shelly and me. I keep telling Shelly, half joking but half proud, "I'm building you a house in the Caribbean." The location is beautiful, but with two small rooms, concrete block walls, a tin roof, little to no electricity, no running water, bucket baths outside and a concrete hole in the ground for a toilet—the luxury of it is open to interpretation.

⌒

A week into the work, on the first of October, as Shelly and I hike home in the afternoon, we find a truck stopped partway up the hill. It's loaded with fifty sacks of cement (one hundred pounds each) and about fifty pieces of iron rebar (each about thirty feet long, bent in half for dragging). The truck can't make it up to our house. The road is still too slippery from last night's downpour. Shelly continues up toward home as I pitch in and drag rebar (four or five pieces at a time for me; eight or ten at a time for the other men) for four trips (about five hundred yards) up the steep, slippery slope. I proudly break my first house-building sweat. Darkness envelops us, and what remains on the truck is unloaded by the side of the road. As the truck begins its descent toward the city, the driver fires three gunshots into the air to announce to anyone who might be tempted that he is planning to defend his truck. I'm nauseous from the work of dragging rebar, but we finish getting it all up to the house. One more trip up the hill and I'll vomit, so I shift to the considerably less heroic job of helping load hundred-pound cement sacks onto the heads or shoulders of three men, including Maxime, who carry them two-thirds of the way up the steep hill to store at a neighbor's house. By the end of the night, the men are glistening in the flashlight, shirts long ago removed, muscles taut, each man dusted from face to waist in the fine gray silt of cement. It must have taken almost two hours, but the cement is safely stored for the night. Jean Louis pays each carrier a purple one-hundred goud note (about $2.50), which they consider not bad for two hours' work since one hundred gouds is standard minimum wage for a full day's labor.

Shelly, at home keeping the dogs from attacking, has been worried by the gunshot blasts issued earlier. I should have sent word to her that everything was fine.

This week profound guilt wells up inside me because we're going to live in a new (if simple) house on a lovely mountainside rather than in a decrepit, rat-ridden shack in Cité Soleil, Haiti's worst slum. According to some, like Mother Teresa, Cité Soleil is among the worst places to live on the planet—so part of me thinks I'll always be cheating unless I'm there (not that we could necessarily survive there). I want to go all the way, but I also want some comfort and compromise. Our marriage is already stumbling under the weight of my (quixotic?) quest. I want and need to offer Shelly safety and security and what is best for her. I also need to experiment with following this love of neighbor where it demands. The simplicity of needs here exposes life's complexities. Naked.

Meanwhile rain has rammed down on our tin roof for long stretches during each of the last three nights. Under the tin roof, since we can't talk, it's like being bathed in loud silence. Clouds gather over the mountains surrounding the city starting at about noon, ready to unleash by sunset. The rain fell especially hard Sunday night. As we walked down the mountain on Monday, it looked like an earthquake had hit the road. Water had collapsed some cliffs and tossed around rocks and carved the dirt into new trenches, new hills. The water cut deep in places. Moonscape. People in the tap-tap on the way into the city said fifteen people further up in the mountains died from the rain last night—mostly from houses collapsing.

At the work site another crew of three men started clearing our land today. Maxime's team had been replaced by Jean Louis because they liked talking more than working. The new team complained about the heavy, rain-soaked dirt and didn't show up for a week. So he found a third team: Rigo, Franzlie and Jasper. They're all compact, powerfully built men who are quick with a joke. Their feet are equipped with flip-flops, black dress loafers with toes peaking out and white sneakers with flapping soles, respectively.

The next morning Rigo, Franzlie and Jasper are out swinging their pick and hoes, and Moïse, a neighbor from down the path, arrives in the front yard to start making blocks. He works with cement, water collected by old oil drums set under our eaves and sand carried by a truck to the end of the path, then carried the rest of the way by bucket. He mixes sand, cement and water together on the ground, then shovels the mix into a metal mold and bangs the top with the back of the shovel to pack it down. He takes the mold over to the side and turns it over, pulls out a slot and releases it onto the ground to dry—like making sand castles on the beach.

Jean Louis wanted him to bring assistants, but Moïse came alone. Another worker whispers, "He wants all the money for himself," before adding what was either his own wisdom or a Haitian proverb: "The man who wants all the money for himself ends up killing himself."

By the end of the day, he has made eighty-six blocks.

⌒

Everyone is calling me "Patron," which feels funny at first, then depressing. I'm in Haiti partly to try to play some tiny part in bettering the situation birthed from the abhorrent patron-slave system. We're building this little house because we want to live with integrity at a similar level to many of our neighbors. Of course, some of our neighbors live five people to a small, unfinished concrete room or in countryside woven wood homes or in the cramped, awful quarters of dangerous slums. We certainly won't have the nicest house in the village; ours should rank somewhere in the middle. On the other hand, I am paying their wages. (We've instructed Jean Louis to pay better than the going rates, but also affordable.)

I don't want to be a white man who has black men carrying heavy loads on their shoulders as they pass me and say, *"Bonjou, patron."* But I am. I don't want to gloss over reality or idealize this experience. Maxime is one of the people who always calls me Patron and refuses to use my name, as in his oft-repeated refrain— sometimes with a plate full of food in his hand—*"Patron, mwen grangou."* "Patron, I'm hungry." And he is very poor, though not often hungry. Maxime's crew was dismissed, but he has hung around to do odd jobs. Today when Maxime complains to me of his hunger with the other guys watching, as he does every day, I try humor: "Maxime, I really need to talk with your wife and make sure she feeds you." Everyone laughs.

Ways to try disarming these charged interactions are (1) try to live with integrity and (2) respond with wit. Neither works all the time, but laughter often bridges to real human interaction. Stumble or show weakness, and often people will sense vulnerable prey who might unload a few dollars to buy his way out of the uncomfortable situation.

‿

A week after blocks start being made, assembly of the iron rebar columns begins. They'll be implanted in the foundation. The lead worker for this part of the project looks like a bigger, more muscular Malcolm X. His name is Wilio. After we're introduced, he says in English, "I work for you"—and then stares into me, unsmiling.

We should finish clearing rock by the end of the week. Then work on the foundation can begin. Rain continues to damage the area, slow our work, cause minor mudslides on our property and major mudslides in the area. We've stopped making blocks since the truck carrying sand can't make it up the washed-out road.

$\frown$

Today, October 17, marks the anniversary of the death of Jean-Jacques Dessalines, a slave brought from Africa who became Haiti's first emperor after the country won its independence two hundred years ago. He later died in an ambush by some of the leaders who had helped him win Haiti's revolution. The current opposition is trying to set a political ambush, hardly a secret, for President Aristide. Aristide is Haiti's first democratically elected leader since its independence. A former Catholic priest who preached liberation theology and came from a poor family, Aristide had been the embodiment of so much hope for the nation when first elected. Disappointment eroded some of his support. Now neither side can agree about new elections. The opposition claims Aristide has become a dictator, not as severe as but still in the tradition of Haiti's most recent tyrants, Papa Doc Duvalier and his son, Baby Doc. The government supporters believe the opposition does not represent the will of the people and is undermining Haiti's fourteen-year-old democracy. Eight people have been killed, thirty-one wounded, in political demonstrations in the past month, mostly in the country's north.

In addition to the national political development in danger of being stunted (or saved, depending on one's perspective), Haiti is littered with the incomplete. Partially completed homes are everywhere. Only about 2 percent of children who start school (and between one-third and one-half never even start) graduate from high school. The projects of international development organizations routinely fail—abandoned because of bad strategy or a lack of will to adjust through the challenges. Thinking of Dessalines's death and the country's development since then, I wonder about our place here. I wonder if our work, our house, our life in Haiti will be something long-term or just another mediocre idea, quickly abandoned, unfinished.

Shelly and I are called to the site this morning for The Tracing, which means outlining the foundation. Eighteen days into October, we're not ahead of schedule, but I'm not sure how far behind we are. The Tracing appears to be of symbolic importance and can't begin without us, so we walk over before work. The tools are a mallet, a ball of string, a tape measure, a square and some cut-up saplings to use as markers to tie the string to. The square is held up to the intersection of strings to ensure each corner is ninety degrees. Wilio, Jean Louis, Pouchon, Jacques, Maxime, Moïse and a few other guys I don't yet know worked on this. This meant nine loudly spoken opinions (plus the two quiet ones of Shelly and me) about how our house should be laid out. In importance, our opinion ranks somewhere in the middle of the group. Each person who visits the site has a strong, specific idea of how things should proceed. The masons are bossing around the land-clearers, who don't like it but do what they're told. The son of the local *hougan* (Vodou priest), who is also a *hougan* in training, drops by. He looks slightly menacing with jagged, blackened teeth—but that's a dental issue, not a spiritual one. He seems like a gentle guy. Jean Louis, in conservative church director mode, teases him, pretends to be possessed by a *lwa* (spirit), and tells him to give up Vodou and attend his church so he can avoid eternal flames. I was the only one who shook hands with him, though it's likely that some of the men have semi-secretly been to his father's house for festivals or healings or advice.

Then this afternoon, after The Tracing, we decide to change the location of the balcony. Shelly saves us from a really bad plan that for some reason had the porch mostly facing a crumbling rock cliff. As we work out the new plan on the site, Shelly at one point lies down on the ground where our bed will be, to sense the room dimensions.

Then Jean Louis starts exclaiming, "This is going to be a fancy house, house of a *gwo neg.*" *Gwo neg* means "big man" or "big shot." He says this because we've decided to extend the front balcony by a meter, thus giving the house six corners rather than the four of a rectangle house with a back porch. He says this will hardly cost

House Under Construction

approx. 20 feet

approx. 20 feet

bed

kitchen and living

barrels to catch rainwater off roof

front porch

path to old house and down to the city

outhouse

any more money, but the two extra corners mark my arrival as a *gwo neg*. He announces this to Maxime and Wilio, Pouchon and Jacques. I don't want this reputation, but is this an impulse to shirk my responsibility in the community?

Maybe he was just stroking my ego and setting me up, because after he explains that the back wall must now be made of rock, not cement block, he slips in, "I think you might not be understanding that the $530 for the supporting rock wall is not included in the house price."

What! So tonight I'm brooding because our house is improving. Shelly's also upset but thinks I'm dumb for feeling guilty over two extra corners, twenty-four more square feet on our front balcony: "Four corners or six, it's still a two-room house with no plumbing and cement floors." Though Shelly sometimes downplays my ideals as whimsical and self-righteous, we share many of the same commitments—and she often ends up living out what I consider the ideal (about money, simplicity, spiritual disciplines and so on) better than I do.

⌒

The rain keeps coming, causing a rockslide last night on our foundation. Rocks and dirt are now piled six feet high right where our bed will be, exactly where Shelly laid on the ground two days ago. The rockslide would have killed any workers who were digging there. This morning workers assure us that the back rock wall of the house will be *janm* (solid) to withstand a small landslide. Suddenly, digging into our savings to spend $530 extra on the back wall, though it will stretch us, doesn't seem like too big a deal. Morning tap-tap conversations continue about which houses collapsed last night, whether anyone died. The rain will not let up. "Thanks for the water, God," someone says on the tap-tap today, "but please give us a little break." Some people say the rain always comes hard in October but hammers like this only every five years. Others say they can't remember it ever being this bad.

I don't sleep well that night. Anxiety wakes me every few hours with her shrill beckoning. *Will our new house collapse on us as we sleep?* The next afternoon I'm bursting with questions (as if I know anything) about the walls, the rebar, the reinforcements, the thickness of the rock wall, whether it can really withstand a rockslide. Wilio is on our front lawn making three-by-three-foot iron grids that will be implanted under the columns in our foundation. Jean Louis asks, "Wilio, did you use these in your house?" Wilio responds directly to me, "You have to for a good house, but I couldn't afford to make them this good, with this much iron. Not like you, *Patron*." My shoulders slump. "Oh."

❧

Shelly and I talk for a long time about life in Haiti and our (hopefully long) lives yet to come. We avoid specifics about construction. We're both frazzled. For two months now, between three and ten men have been in front of, behind and going past our house before and after work. This, after needing recuperation from our good but utterly unprivate seven months in Woshdlo. Our current latrine in the back is a concrete hole in the ground that one squats over, with sheets of tin on one side and full exposure on the other three sides. Shelly's been going to the bathroom before the workers arrive or after they leave. But they come at dawn and leave at dusk. A few mornings ago one of the workers accidentally saw her in the latrine, a vulnerable position to say the least. She came into the house crying. Several times I've stood out beside her holding up a sheet for privacy. This is absurd. I feel awful for her. I'm an idiot. At minimum I need to solve the latrine problem today.

❧

A couple of days later Jean Louis, Wilio, Rigo, a few other guys and I sit sipping rum on the balcony in the late afternoon to escape rain. Wilio's girlfriend is three months pregnant. Wilio says, "Yes, I sinned against the Holy Spirit . . . but, you know, we've been together for six years! I'm still with the Holy Spirit, but I'm also with her. But now that she's pregnant, I can't take Communion in church till I'm married. Can't marry till I finish building my house." He seems completely sincere about his sin and unapologetic about his love. Everyone laughs, teases, sips.

⌒

The iron columns were placed today, Saturday, October 25. There is now a four-foot-thick, rock-and-cement foundation in place that hugs into the cutaway cliff. Nine rust-colored rebar columns are set around the foundation and reach nine feet in the air. Everyone was thankful because not one cloud dotted the blue sky. Four guys (one barefoot) carried sacks of sand up the slippery path and then another hundred yards back to the site for six hours straight. Wilio and a colleague put in the columns.

In the morning I had gone down to work while Shelly stayed home. Partway down my hike to get a tap-tap, our neighbor Sonson drove by (the only one nearby who has a vehicle, a four-by-four) and offered me a ride to the city. Sonson is working on a house in the city for his uncle, so we talked construction. On that project, he had a bad mason: "He would take money for ten sacks of cement, buy five, pocket the rest."

As we drove, Sonson stopped to pick up a different mason, Amos, who lives near us, to take him to look at the job. Amos said sure and climbed in the back of the old Land Cruiser. Sonson described the job and slipped in that another mason, who wasn't honest, had been on the job but needed replacing. "Whoa! Whoa! No! Stop the car!" Amos said. Sonson braked. We were next to the local cemetery, full of small concrete squares that each hold four to six coffins. "People die for this," Amos said as he climbed out of the truck. "No, no, I won't take his job." He started walking back up the hill. We kept driving down. Sonson shook his head. "It's their principle. They never take someone else's job. Too dangerous."

"So what will you do?" I asked.

"I have to get that dishonest mason to find someone else to do the job, to replace himself." The working class finds small ways to try to protect itself.

I returned home at noon and stayed occupied keeping the three dogs from attacking the men each time they passed. I helped carry a few loads back to the site. Later in the afternoon, as the work finished, a torrential downpour unleashed. Wilio, Pouchon, Jacques, Manno, Maxandre and Jean quickly made their way to our porch. In the noise we could only sit quietly. The temperature quickly dropped. I noticed a few men shivering. I went in for the rum, my cultural crutch. The older mason, a Protestant, didn't partake. Others were grateful, saying it helps them *chofe* (warm up). After an hour and a half the rain lightened, and they headed home.

⌒

Couldn't sleep last night. Rubbing my eyes as I arrive on the site, I find Jean Louis asking Wilio whether he understands how condoms work. Wilio looks a little annoyed. I say, "So, Jean Louis, were you married before you had your kids?" Wilio jumps in: "No, they weren't married!" Jean Louis looks away and says, "Yes, but we don't tell people that." Wilio laughs, "But everyone knows."

The three of us talk about house plans, but I'm so tired that Creole is senseless to me. During the long discussion they occasionally pause, turn to me and say, "That's what you want, right?" "Um, yes," I say, because it's the easiest, quickest answer. Tomorrow I need to find out what I've agreed to. Also, yesterday Jean Louis said, "I don't think we're going to have any rocks left for when we get to building the back wall after the foundation is finished." Translation: five hundred dollars more. I really need to corner him on money, but he perplexes my attempts at specificity. Houses are generally built in protracted stages in Haiti, so I'm coming to the clear but worrying conclusion that Jean Louis has no idea how to figure costs in advance. Normally you just see how far the money you have will take you. Then stop. When you find a little more money, you do another stage. The process, attested to by all the unfinished houses and by conversations with people we know, can easily take two, five or ten years. In Woshdlo we watched a neighbor begin building an outhouse. The hole was dug in several stages over about eight weeks, then it was left until there was enough money to buy sand. After the sand, they would wait for the money to buy cement. And so on. When I asked, they optimistically said they should have a new latrine in about two years.

We've also been told that building in stages like this functions as a sort of a savings account, where most can't get a mortgage or wouldn't put money in a bank, because once you build a stage, then you don't have cash when a sibling or cousin inevitably comes to you with a financial emergency. If you waited to build until you had all the money in hand, you would never have enough. You would always have to be dipping into your money to help out with crises. Culturally, people often don't marry until they have a house (Wilio's situation). But because it can take so long, many have children before they're married. Otherwise life is put on hold permanently for lack of funds. The fiancée/wife and kid(s) live with her family until the husband can build a house.

⌒

This afternoon, the last day of October, includes a three-hour wait at the airport for a friend who never arrives. On leaving the airport, we get stuck in an awful traffic jam because robbers are shooting out the tires of bank vehicles and Western Union–type cars on Rue Delmas, one of the city's main roads. We hit several more traffic jams. Then in a riverbed on the way up our mountain, we get stuck. A few guys push us out for fifty gouds. Then we run out of gas. The driver, a Haitian friend who lives down in the city, gets the attention of a passing car. Then he rolls back down the road to look for gas as we run to catch a ride with strangers, who drop us off in the dark where the paved road ends and most vehicles can't go higher. It is now pouring.

We're in shorts and T-shirts, with no flashlight or umbrella. We're basically walking blind. The path is treacherous; I've fallen on a sunny afternoon before. We're moving up over loose rocks, and the road has turned into an eight-inch-deep rushing river. Never have I been so at the capricious mercy of nature. Occasionally Shelly is crawling on all fours. We somehow make it without spraining an ankle, propelled upward by adrenaline. We dry off, put on dry clothes, pour a generous rum for Jean Louis (yes, he was there waiting for us in the dark). We recount our adventure. Jean Louis smiles and then, barely visible in the lamplight, says, "We're out of rocks, but the foundation is done."

DUST TO DUST, BUT WATER IN BETWEEN

We must risk delight. We can do without pleasure,
but not delight. Not enjoyment. We must have
the stubbornness to accept our gladness in the ruthless
furnace of this world. To make injustice the only
measure of our attention is to praise the Devil.

JACK GILBERT, "A BRIEF FOR THE DEFENSE"

Outside, standing naked in a small, dented metal basin, shivering and dripping after bathing scoop by scoop out of a small bucket, I sometimes enviously imagine stepping out of a tub after a long, hot shower to dry off in thickly humid air in front of a steamed-up mirror. But without running water and with scarce electricity (a few hours every few days), we bathe as our neighbors do.

During the day the lack of privacy because of our construction project is maddening and especially hard on Shelly. But at night after all the workers have gone home and when we're not frustrated with each other, we both find something sublimely satisfying about bathing bare and unashamed surrounded by the private company of coconut, grapefruit and avocado trees lit by a single kerosene lamp.

The Bible reminds us in its first few chapters that from dust we come and to dust we shall return. In between, though, we're largely water (about 60 percent of the body). I had never felt this ninth-grade biology fact *existentially* during my typical daily routine of showering in the morning, shaving (yes, sometimes with the faucet running), multiple toilet flushings, running the dishwasher, taking an afternoon shower after working out, doing a load of laundry and so on. But for our first seven months in Woshdlo, Shelly and I carried each gallon of water we used about a hundred yards from the nearest tap. Remarkable how quickly the heart can convert to conservationism.

Now we live where the water is even farther away and our work schedule is fuller, so we pay a teenage neighbor named Beebee to get water for us every couple of days (which helps him pay high-school tuition and buy books). Our household (Shelly, me, the three dogs who provide nighttime security and of course Mitsu, who provides rat security) consumes about five gallons of water per day—to bathe, wash dishes, cook and drink. When the rain falls, we capture it in discarded oil drums set up under our eaves. We use water from the local spring for cooking and drinking, but rainwater for everything else. Our consumption is in line with the daily average for rural Haitians (somewhere under two-and-a-half gallons per person), whereas the average American consumes about 150 gallons daily (see my routine above).

Our area has easier access to water than some other places in Haiti, where people walk three hours to the nearest source. But still the situation is fragile. During a recent dry spell before the October rains, the local spring dried up. To get a few gallons of water, people hiked forty arduous, mountain minutes to the nearest supply. Overextended, that supply's flow gradually lessened to a trickle, rippling out fear that it too would run dry. Suddenly life became a daily battle just to keep from turning back into dust.

Thankfully, the heavens eventually tired of their stinginess and rain fell for a week straight. One afternoon we passed our local source to find it bustling with fifty women and children waiting their turn to fill gallon jugs, indulging in an occasional playful splash on a friend, smiling, bathing, scrubbing their clothes. Never could I have guessed such a scene would make me so happy.

Another thing that makes me happy is—now that winter has brought a relative chill to our mountainside (evenings probably in the mid sixties Fahrenheit)—we've started heating a little bath water on our small gas burner to take the edge off. It's amazing what becomes luxurious.

BUILDING A HOME (PART II)

See how the siege ramps are built up to take the city.

JEREMIAH 32:24

The ancient prophet Jeremiah was, not surprisingly, under arrest in his native Jerusalem. The city was under siege by the powerful Babylonian army, but instead of rallying the people to strength, hope and national security, Jeremiah instead tromped around declaring, "This is what the LORD says: I am about to hand this city over to the king of Babylon, and he will capture it. Zedekiah king

of Judah will not escape. . . . If you fight . . . you will not succeed"
(Jeremiah 32:3-5). Not helpful.

But then while Jeremiah was still under arrest in the king's
courtyard, God let him know he was about to get an offer that—
despite better business sense—he should accept. Jeremiah's cousin
comes and says, "Buy my field at Anathoth in the territory of Ben-
jamin" (v. 8), which must have sounded a bit like one Iraqi saying
to another, "I've got a great bridge to sell you in Baghdad" during
the countdown to the U.S. invasion. But in an action of defiant
hope, Jeremiah weighs out seven ounces of silver and pays his
cousin. Then, as he accepts the deed for his new land in front of a
group of witnesses, Jeremiah declares: "For this is what the LORD
Almighty, the God of Israel, says: Houses, fields and vineyards
will again be bought in this land" (v. 15).

Our situation is certainly not an exact parallel with Jeremiah's,
and of course Port-au-Prince cannot just be substituted for Jerusalem. Yet it is unsettling that each month as our new house goes up,
the political situation further deteriorates around us. There is a
sort of personal, devotional resonance with the Jeremiah story.

I want to side with defiant hope. I didn't and don't want to build
on the Cayman Islands or the Bahamas or Key West. I want to
hope and build in this place, in Haiti—right here—because I want
desperately for people here to be buying and selling land, working
good jobs, building their own solid homes and a better country. I
want to believe that God will ensure—in whatever inscrutable
ways—that this happens. "Nothing is too hard for you," Jeremiah
goes on to pray after taking the deed (v. 17). I want to echo that
prayer in the face of all the evidence.

But the evidence is more daunting by the day. The pressure is
closing in around President Aristide. After his alleged malfeasance
in the 2000 elections, international countries and institutions
have cut off five hundred million dollars in grants and loans,
tightening the already crushing vise on this nation. The UN De-

velopment Program recently dropped Haiti's "world human development" ranking among nations from 146 to 150. (This isn't the first place that comes to mind with the phrase "Caribbean getaway.") The opposition—a disparate coalition held together by their desire to rid the country of Aristide—is gaining momentum, refusing to compromise and hold new elections unless the president steps down. Government talks with the opposition coalition are going nowhere, with (understandably) no trust on either side in this winner-take-all, loser-fear-for-your-life political culture. Ever harsher rhetoric and occasional violence pile onto already crippling problems of economy, ecology, health, corruption and on and on.

In recent weeks anti-government demonstrations in Gonaïves and the northern city of Cap-Haïtien have seen violent clashes with police that have so far left fourteen dead and more than fifty wounded. Truth is becoming ever more slippery, partisan and dangerous. Journalists have been assassinated and threatened for many years already. The New York–based Committee to Protect Journalists has declared Haiti the second most dangerous country for journalists in the Western Hemisphere, after Colombia. Amiot Métayer, a longtime supporter of President Aristide and head of the "Cannibal Army" gang (villains to many, heroes to some) in Gonaïves, was found shot through each eye and his heart. The gang accused government henchmen of the murder. Though it seems unlikely anyone will be able to force Aristide from power, Métayer's gang and supporters have since taken to vociferously calling for Aristide's ouster. The opposition is trying to build "siege ramps . . . up against the city."

These days Jeremiah-type hope for the future ("Houses, fields and vineyards will again be bought in this land" [32:15] and "I will settle them in safety" [v. 37 NRSV]) is hard to muster and seems an awfully unstable foundation for building a little, concrete-block house—let alone a home or a country.

⌒

It's November 2. Wilio is in our front lawn digging up rocks to use in the back wall. Jean Louis drops by before church. Shelly makes us all grilled cheese sandwiches. As we chew, Wilio says he's working especially hard for us—"Look, even on Sundays." I say I'm grateful but suggest he's probably doing it more to be able to marry his fiancée than for me. He laughs and agrees. "No pride here. I'll do masonry, work with iron, find rocks. I just need money so that in May I can please both my fiancée and God with a wedding."

After a tense start, we're becoming friends. I join him on the search for rocks. We find a few more. He tosses a watermelon-sized rock that lands on the pile with a sharp crack. He looks up and says, "Kent, now that you're going to have a house, it's time to have some children. You'd better get to work."

The foundation is almost finished. (It actually wasn't quite done last week.) Jean Louis asks for $500 to do payroll on Wednesday and to bring up more sand. I say, "Only after we've talked budget." We battle to a grand total for the last stage, the back rock wall, the latrine (somehow this was not part of the original price either) and his services. He said $250 would be fine as his payment, but he said it so it was clear that a little more would be appropriate. We're happy to pay him $450, part of which will help to buy his wife a sewing machine. She's taking a part-time tailoring course at a local Baptist church. And we've started a relationship with his family, which means we'll probably be helping out occasionally for a long time to come. The current grand total will be $4,750.

We're withdrawing from our small savings in the States. We would rather be giving this budget overrun to someone who needs the money. There are tears of fear and frustration from Shelly. We're still unsure of our lives in Haiti. She's given up more than I have to move here but has yet to find her footing. We're investing more money and effort than she's ready to. The house is symbolically and financially tying us long term to a place that she's barely ready to stay in short term. But we're locked in, without other good options.

By the end of the week, two anti-Aristide demonstrations have been broken up by rock-throwing supporters of the president. Aristide's supporters claim the opposition is trying to undermine Haiti's democratically elected leader. The privately owned Radio Caraibes, a popular station, was sprayed with gunfire.

And the block walls of our house have shot up. It took weeks and weeks of chipping away rock and dirt, molding cement blocks, slowly clipping and tying together iron posts to anchor the columns, digging up canals for the foundation, and setting the foundation with rocks and cement. Then after three days of laying blocks, it suddenly looks like a house. It's not quite rebuilding the temple, but about eight hundred blocks went up in a flurry with two teenagers carrying sand, two men carrying blocks and water, one mixing cement, and two laying the blocks. Wilio organized the work. There will be two doors, two windows in the bedroom and one in the other room (though it appears an unplanned second window has been added). The doors and windows will be metal.

When I was helping on the site, Wilio called one of the men mixing cement to come over. It was Pouchon. He's gentle mannered and has stained teeth sticking out at a forty-five-degree angle. "He's forty," Wilio said, "and he's never been with a woman. He hasn't been with a man either. Doesn't like either."

"Um, really?" I said. Everyone laughed. Pouchon just smiled, trying to keep his teeth in his mouth, then went back to mixing cement.

On Thursday, I had Jean Louis come to our office to pick up $1,180, an amount that is safest to deal with in secret. I had sent a motorcycle courier friend, who can't be easily followed, to get it from the bank. I firmly told Jean Louis that this was all, manage it from here. I seriously doubt this will work, but it will make me feel strong and decisive for a few days till the next request.

∽

Today is a payday. It's Saturday. We're at home. Shelly and I were not invited to complicate things by being around. We're at John and Merline's place while Jean Louis and the workers are back at the site. The universal opinion is that it's better for everyone in- volved (and the house) if we stay a step back. Wilio was first to be paid. Manno, the sand hauler, was last in line. Not surprisingly, we heard occasional heated exchanges. Then at the end of three vigorous hours of negotiating, we heard yelling.

Manno arrives upset at our house: He was underpaid! He is al- most crying, this strong, solid twenty-year-old. I feel sick. Is this because we're pressuring Jean Louis to finish within (the latest) budget? The lowest on the social ladder always take the brunt here. He's worked hard. Barefoot. Nice kid. What can we do with- out undermining Jean Louis and reaping a wave of havoc for the rest of the project?

I call Manno back after he's disappeared down the trail and say, "I'll talk with Jean Louis; I'm not in on the money details." Then I pour him a nice glass of rum. After Manno leaves, Jean Louis ap- pears, shaking his head: "This morning Manno said I owed him 100 gouds, then this afternoon he says 775 gouds. I bet someone told him, 'If you're working for a *blan,* then you better get more money out of it.'" Who knows what's true?

Jacques is the oldest worker; he mixes cement and carries water. (I catch myself marveling at him. Underneath the wizened face of a fifty-something-year-old peasant is the body of an Olympic ath- lete.) Suddenly he comes around the house corner, also on the verge of tears: "I lost five hundred gouds. I just moved my cow to a different field and lost the money somewhere." Five hundred gouds was half his pay. Jean Louis goes back to search with him; they don't find it. When Jean Louis returns, I say how sorry I feel for the guy. What can I do? "Oh, he didn't lose it," Jean Louis laughs. "He probably owes someone money but doesn't want his wife to know. This way she'll be angry with him for losing it, but not as angry as if she found out he has to pay off an old debt she didn't know about."

At dusk Jean Louis drops by again after talking with Manno's family. I imagine he both cares about Manno and needs to quickly protect himself and his reputation. They said Manno gets ornery when he drinks, and we should never give him alcohol. He was drinking before he came for his pay (a situation I hardly helped later with my peace offering). Manno had admitted to Jean Louis that he hadn't earned what he'd been demanding and said he'd be back on the job Monday. Clouds are amassing. Jean Louis and I set up the oil drums to catch rainwater. He heads home up the mountain. Rain pours down.

The next morning Shelly and I attend the local Catholic church, a blue and white building perched on a hilltop ten minutes away, which we've come to love. We're both Protestant, but our closest neighbors attend this church, and we've found Haitian Catholic churches here a more natural fit for us. Many Haitian Protestant churches seem very 1950s Southern Baptist (if a little more lively). Most, influenced by missionaries, have rejected their own melodies and traditional drum (associated with Vodou) for ancient European hymns, which here lack spirit compared to the uniquely beautiful Creole melodies and traditional drumming incorporated into Catholic worship services. Protestant churches often read Scripture in French, which Shelly (and most of the congregation) doesn't understand, whereas Vatican II led to Catholic churches doing the entire service in Creole.

This afternoon during post-church neighborly visits, everyone in Mòn Zaboka is talking about a man up the mountain who was digging for sand in his yard yesterday when the hole collapsed on him and he died. People had warned him, but he waved them off. We're digging a hole for our outhouse. So far Rigo has dug five feet down, but Jean Louis assures me there's no danger because Rigo is working in rocky, solid ground. With Wilio banned from church till he marries, he worked half a day today, pouring cement for three of the house's nine columns.

~

Then Monday morning as we prepare to go down to work, Pouchon is bitten on the thigh by one of the dogs. We run out and apologize. "No, don't apologize," says Wilio. "It's good when your dogs are mean! Though it is better if they don't bite the men working here." Wilio's other assistant, Jacques, agrees. Shelly cleans the wound with hydrogen peroxide. Pouchon says it's no big deal. We'll keep an eye on it and pay for him to go to the doctor to get shots.

On the way down the mountain, we pass four men carrying up a beige, lacquered coffin for the man whose sand hole collapsed. As I walk through the city, two older women come up and ask for money. I say, "Sorry, not this time," since I don't have change. Unsatisfied, one of them says to me, "You look just like Jesus did, so I think you should give."

The next day, Tuesday, Jean Louis sends a chaperone to ensure Pouchon actually gets the tetanus and rabies shots (about five hundred gouds, or thirteen dollars). Otherwise it might have been too tempting for him to skip the shots and keep the money for seemingly more pressing needs.

~

On Wednesday Wilio and his colleague stand on the scaffolding of a splintered plank that balances between a window opening on one side and three concrete blocks stacked atop an oil drum on the other side. The plank, which also holds the rocks they're using to build the back wall, is bowed dangerously. Jacques heaves another large rock onto it. Ten feet away another man straddles the newly poured crossbeams of the porch, hammering off the planks that held the concrete in place for twenty-four hours to dry. Mortar is splashed up their forearms and freckles their faces. When I arrive with rum, everyone takes only a brief pause to throw it back and say, "Thank you! Now you watch. The rum gives us strength to work fast!" Rigo, who is twenty feet down in the latrine hole with a pick and a shovel, shirtless and shoeless in baggy Tommy Hilfiger jean shorts, comes up for a drink. His young assistant pauses from hoisting up buckets of dirt and rock with a rope.

In the afternoon when we return, there's a pile of white, chalky stones on the roadside down the path from our house, just delivered by truck from the dry riverbed below. Three guys are moving them from the roadside up into the neighbors' *lakou* so nobody steals them during the night. I step into the line passing the rocks from down below up to the pile. Forty-five minutes into the work, three young men come sprinting down the road. "Wilio, come talk with me," one says.

"No, I'm working."

"Come talk with me. Now." Wilio goes over and talks by the side of the dirt road. Then he stands silently, alone, as the three men continue hurrying down. After a few minutes he speaks quietly with Jean Louis. He looks off down the mountain.

I ask what's wrong. "A little problem," Wilio says quietly. He pitches in to help move a few more rocks, then walks off. I ask Jean Louis. "His brother's been shot down in the city."

After we finish moving rocks and the other workers leave, Jean Louis tells me the story of how he'd nearly been killed by Wilio's brother five years ago. (Wilio and his brother are cousins of Jean Louis's wife.) Jean Louis and Wilio's brother had been arguing in front of the house where Shelly and I are staying. Wilio's brother attacked Jean Louis. He choked him and struck him on the head with a rock. Threw his body off the small retaining wall. Somehow (he can't really remember it), Jean Louis crawled his way through the trees down to the road and collapsed. People found him just as Wilio's brother returned with a machete to finish the job. That was five years ago. Now this brother lies in a hospital down in the city. No one knows how serious his condition is.

Today's other news is that the pro-government station Radio Pyramid was set on fire and destroyed in the city of Saint-Marc.

At about 11:30 p.m. Shelly and I awake to the sound of women's agonizing cries piercing the darkness. We lie motionless in bed. Finally one of us whispers, "He died."

<hr />

Wilio's brother did die last night. No one worked this morning, but about half the guys came by. We sat around in our yard talking quietly. Jean Louis is the general contractor, but Wilio is the heart of the project. Apparently his brother had gone to a bank in Port-au-Prince to cash a check to distribute for payroll at a job he was working on. When he left the bank, he was followed, shot, robbed. You hear stories like this regularly as the political situation and general security worsen. Downtown today hundreds of university students and opposition activists demonstrated in front of the National Palace. They and pro-government supporters threw rocks at each other. Violent clashes are increasing in cities like Cap-Haïtien and Gonaïves. Police are using tear gas. Aristide is vowing to continue as president for two more years to finish his five-year term (which ends in early 2006). Tension is ratcheted up by each protest, each person's death.

We give Jean Louis payroll money ahead of schedule so he can give Wilio an advance to pay for his brother's funeral. We also give extra, as is expected of us as his employer, to help with the funeral expenses. We stay home today. There are calls for a general strike against the government to protest the violence against protesters. When political discussions break out among neighbors or fellow tap-tap passengers, we just listen, ask questions, stay neutral. The country's political direction is not for us to decide.

⌒

We're out of sand. We're way over budget. The money I gave Jean Louis as a final installment is spent. It's Tuesday, November 18, and everything stops. The walls are almost done. Down the center of the house runs a small cement canal that will catch rainwater on our tin roof (which will be shaped like a V) and send it out one side into our old, red and black Texaco oil barrels. We didn't want this canal, but our vote isn't binding. Several workers just spent three days making archlike curves (instead of just leaving them at ninety-degree angles) where the columns on the porch meet the concrete crossbeams—an unnecessary decorative flourish.

I ask Jean Louis how much sand we need to finish the house. We calculate. We trim some of his ideas. My approach, with new-found and expensive cultural insight, is, "Okay, maybe we can do that eventually, but let's *not* do any of that till we first finish these few things. Then we'll see if we have leftover materials." Sounds good, he says, and then admits the materials might not quite stretch that far. I feel proud of myself. Prioritizing might work better than just saying no—or trying to calculate parallel expenses. Our compromised priorities are (1) finish the roof, (2) cement the floor, (3) cement the inside walls and (4) finish the outhouse. (We're now going to enclose the outhouse with tin, which will be cheaper than cement.) Finally Jean Louis says, "You know I didn't have the outside of my house cemented before I moved in; almost nobody does. Maybe after a couple years you can do the extras.

But we've done a great first stage of construction!"

Progress, however, is not being made toward political compromise. Quite the opposite. A recent political study of Haiti by Robert Fatton Jr., a University of Virginia professor from Haiti, is titled *Haiti's Predatory Republic: The Unending Transition to Democracy.* The way things are playing out seem consistent with his analysis. The current clash is over who holds power in the National Palace, but the underlying instability is chronic, seemingly intractable and much deeper: "Haiti's predatory democracy is thus the result of . . . the persisting legacy of a dictatorial habitus, and . . . the fragility and indeed virtual absence of both a productive bourgeoisie and a large working class." Then later, "While material want and the ugly struggle for necessity are not absolute obstacles to democratic rule and effective collective action, they tend to favor the emergence of tyrants and populist demagogues." The predators are those who hold power, as they go after the nation's scarce resources. The prey? Well, they're the same people as always.

⌒

The next afternoon Jean Louis and I attend Wilio's brother's funeral. It's the first Haitian funeral I've been to, though I've attended several wakes. We can't get inside the church—too many people—so we stand outside with a couple hundred others. When the singing stops, the casket is closed. Suddenly the hysterical screaming of women rips the heavy silence. One by one, women and family members are ushered out, supported on either side, barely able to walk, their bodies spent on sorrow.

Toward the end of the procession, surrounded by people, Wilio comes down the stairs just ahead of the casket, singing at the top of his lungs, his voice raspy and cracking:

They killed my big brother.
They killed my big brother.

They shot him with a gun.

Good Lord, they killed my big brother.

They took him away from me . . .

He sings this over and over, with his powerful arms draped over the shoulders of friends on either side of him. My body shivers with sadness. I feel his brother's death in the pit of my stomach, though I never met him. It is the most eloquent, beautiful, heart-rending expression of grief I've ever experienced.

Sunday morning Jean Louis comes by. The forty-eight pieces of wood he bought to serve as crossbeams are fourteen feet long instead of sixteen. Now we must find a few long beams to anchor down the coming improvisation. Jean Louis and I cut down a tall, straight tree nearby that will be a perfect beam. As we do, he tells me that recently Rigo had told him to hold his wages for a few weeks so Rigo could save up for his wife and child to move back to their hometown of Jérémie, a southern coastal town about ten hours away. Rigo would visit them but needs to stay here where he can find semi-regular work. But then last night Rigo's two-year-old niece, his brother's daughter, died unexpectedly. (Later Rigo said she hadn't been sick, just slightly asthmatic.) So at 5:00 this morning, Rigo woke up Jean Louis to ask for his meager savings plus an advance so he could help his brother with the funeral. I've met his brother several times, and Shelly and I will give money to help. I was talking about how sad the girl's death was and how hard it is to get ahead. Jean Louis said, *"Oui, mais c'est la vie."*

A couple of days later, halfway through his workday, the guy who had taken over Manno's job of carrying sand demands more than double his agreed-upon pay because he is doing the work for a *blan*. The fee for lifting a truckload of sand jumped instantly from 350 gouds to 750 gouds. Jean Louis says no. Jean Louis tells everyone (they've all grown up together) that the project is his, that they're working for him, not us. We're starting to hear rumors of a rift between the workers and Jean Louis. I'm sure there's so much happening that we don't understand.

◦—

I'm exhausted. Only a few days left in November. After finishing work, Shelly and I are hiking up to home. I hoped to put my nose-stuffed, head-pounding, lung-shrunk body to bed by 7 p.m. But there sitting on our porch in the late afternoon sun is . . . please, no . . . yes, it's Jean Louis. I say hi and then hear, *"Ann ale."* "Let's go." A command, not a question.

Excuse the melodrama, but everything has been feeling more dramatic lately. We haven't personally been too close to any demonstrations, but it's what everyone is talking about. And not too far away, bullets and guns and pepper gas and tear gas and—honestly—poison-ivy spiked water are flying through the air. Various leaders are targeted for murder. Rhetoric ratchets up.

We wind into the woods. Jean Louis announces, "We're finding two trees so work on the crossbeams can continue tomorrow." For forty-five minutes we stumble, crouch and slip up and down the mountainside. I ask, "What about that tree?" Not the right kind of wood. "That one?" No, not tall or straight enough. (It needs to be at least twelve inches in diameter, and tall enough to produce a twenty-foot beam.) "That one," I say, pointing at the silhouette of a perfect, thirty-foot, straight-as-an-arrow tree. "It's perfect," he says, "but, no, it's not on my land . . . though Edwa is a cousin. Well, maybe. Okay, we'll give him the avocado trees we had to cut. The wood's dry, so he can use them for cooking." Arriving at the tree, we find it is hiding its twin, but we reluctantly agree it wouldn't be right to take both. Jean Louis hacks with his machete. I ensure the tree falls downhill so it won't pull down the live electrical wires strung through the branches from tree to tree. Jean Louis chops off its branches. We carry our prize. I'm dizzy but hopeful. The moon lights our way. Fifteen more minutes of "What about that one?" until we find another perfect beam . . . on the same neighbor's land. "We have to work fast," Jean Louis looks around and says, as he starts chopping. Then he says, "When Edwa is thirsty and passes by your new house, you'll give him a glass of water, right?" Sure. He hacks more, then pauses, looks up. "You won't mind if Edwa comes and sits on your porch during a rainstorm, right?" Of course not. Then I realize he is assembling points to sweeten our offer in what will surely be a boisterous after-the-fact negotiating session in the next few days. "Careful with that little tree," Jean Louis says. "Someday someone's going to need it like we need this one." I suggest it will be perfect some-day for his eleven-year-old son, Titi. Jean Louis likes the idea. We lay the second tree down at the site and say good night.

Construction malaise is slugging through my veins. Shelly is unhappy with the house, with the price, with living in Haiti, with me. I don't foresee how this finishes with both of us happy. One weight that is heavier on her than me is the hospitality expecta-tion. The woman patron of the project is expected to provide food; the man provides rum and money. But Shelly works (now coordi-nating our organization's cultural exchange programs), whereas normally there would be a few women in the *lakou* who would take care of this during the day. We provide extra money for them to buy food, but frequently workers still say indignantly to her, "What, you're leaving the house? You're not making us rice today?"

We're trying to live like this and build like this partly to act with integrity and gain respect in our community. We're trying to live like this so we can better understand people's reality and thus better work for them. Instead, Shelly gets insulted for not fulfilling expectations that are impossible for her to meet. And I cringe to imagine the frequency of our cultural blunders.

The tension of walking through streets in a fracturing society each day certainly bleeds over into our personal life. More clashes in Gonaïves again today. This protest marked the shooting of three students eighteen years ago by Jean-Claude Duvalier's army. Outrage over the incident was apparently part of what brought down Baby Doc.

⌒

The roof crew starts early, tacking five-by-three-foot sheets of corrugated tin onto the crossbeams. All three are wearing tattered, button-down shirts, slacks and beat-up dress shoes as they balance around on the walls and beams. No hard hats, safety lines or OSHA regulations.

Rigo mentions that a couple of days ago, down in the city, he had to dive to the street to avoid getting shot in crossfire.

When I return from the city after work, Shelly says a neighbor has been here to ask whether we're coming to the baptism party for Maxime's child, which we'd been invited to a month ago and reminded of often since. I'd forgotten. Shelly and I quickly walk past the house site (it's got a tin roof!), down through the ravine, over the path and up to the house Maxime rents. Almost everyone is already gone, just a few family members left. But they're happy to see us. They had set aside for us plates of the standard celebration meal of deep-fried plantains, fried chicken, beet salad, tangy coleslaw and rice and beans. Delicious food. Maxime shows us his house. He, his wife, their two kids and Manno sleep in a room slightly smaller than the smallest room in our new house, with one double bed in it. His cousin's family lives in the other room of the house. Their *lakou* is on a hilltop with a clear view overlooking Port-au-Prince. You can see downtown, the ports, out onto the Caribbean. We dance a bit, tell stories, laugh. As we leave, they say we'll have to come up and hang out with them at sunset. It's beautiful as the sun goes down. The city sparkles with light.

Two days later I return from church to find that Edwa had been there yelling at—not really at, but to—Shelly about the fact that his trees were stolen: "It was no good! Maybe if they'd asked first! No, it's not Kent I have a problem with, it's Jean Louis! Kent's only an accomplice. Jean Louis needs to come talk with me! It's his responsibility to find me!" The anger is probably part bluster, designed for the fun of the confrontation and to extract better compensation, but I'm still glad it's Jean Louis who will be dealing with him, not me.

⌒

Work on the house continued during December's first several weeks. John and Merline returned, so our house-sitting was finished, and Shelly and I flew to the United States and Canada for two weeks over Christmas and New Year's Day (Haiti's bicentennial) to see our families. Our new house looked like a house but wasn't yet livable. The country was also becoming increasingly unlivable for many, with demonstrations now having claimed at least twenty-two lives, with many more wounded, since mid-September. We flew north, assured the house would be ready when we returned but knowing it wouldn't be.

It wasn't. We returned to our little plot in Mòn Zaboka to find that the front and back porches, as well as the outside block wall, were not yet cemented. The electric work hadn't started. Forty-two had now died in political violence. We slept in the office in Port-au-Prince for a week as they painted the interior walls of our house white and finished cementing the floor. The city is as intense as ever.

After borrowing a bed, a table and two chairs from John and Merline, we moved in. I carried Shelly across the threshold of our first house. We were relieved, but it was anticlimactic. The house was damp and bare. My clear-visioned, Jeremiah-like fervor has gone a little soggy.

THREE SCENES OF FEAR AND IMPROBABLE VENGEANCE

Q: Are you scared living here?

A: No. I mean, it's not the wild, primitive place some people imagine it to be. But yes, sure there's fear. I recently saw a charred body lying on the side of the road—murdered, burned alive, left there—but everyone else I see every day is alive. So I don't know what the odds are, how Vegas would tease out the probabilities, how much fear is justified. I'm here, want to be here, don't want to be elsewhere. There's also a tightness in my stomach that never releases.

Q: Does it . . .

A: But I still laugh. I mean, I laugh from deeper down in my belly than ever before, maybe right from the same place where it's tense. The most insightful part of Graham Greene's novel on Haiti is probably the title: *The Comedians*. It's more brilliant the more I understand life here, the more my respect for people grows. I think of the title when I pass people bargaining in the street market. Or when I see people about to go angrily at each other's throats and then burst into laughter and slap backs. Or during conversations on the porch with friends who have no choice but to ram continuously into life's absurdities. Or when conversations easily ricochet off God, bounce into teasing a neighbor, dive into death's sadness, mention the inability to pay for the kids' school, rebound with lewd sexual innuendo and finish with a sincere statement that everything is in God's hands—all in about three minutes. The best comedy bumps up against the tragic, right? Otherwise it's superficial and touches nothing real.

Q: So how do people manage their fears? How do you?

A: I've found no capacity to *manage* fear. Sadness is different, right? Sadness loses some of its strangling grip over time, gives back ever so slightly the ability to draw oxygen. Fear you can't manage. I mean, well, I don't want to make broad claims, but many Haitians participate in a bustling, powerful and real spiritual world that, among other things, seems to give people some sense of control over their fears and fate. Americans and Canadians, we go to church or to a therapist or to war. But different than sadness, fear gains a tighter hold with each day. Yes, you can get a little numb to it, you just have to keep living, but meanwhile it keeps burrowing down deeper into your stomach, burrowing further up into your imagination. It doesn't tightly grip every moment of every day. But when occasionally it flexes, the fear is way too vivid. And unavoidable.

Q: For instance?

A: There are scenes I've imagined, though I try as hard as I can to chase them away . . .

⌒

Scene One. Behind the group of men is a rusting, light green Daihatsu missing its front tires; the windshield is plywood, plastic bags and lots of tape. He stands six feet tall, muscles straining against his beige slacks and tight, navy blue tank top, talking with three friends beside the rumpled dirt and rock road that she and I walk regularly on the way down the mountain to Port-au-Prince. An argument about when we're next going home to visit family in the States ended with her walking silently a few steps ahead of me. So I watch as she passes just in front of him. He stares into her with cold concentration, puckers his lips, then makes a long, sloppy mmmmmmppp smooch while nodding his chin up slightly and lifting his left eyebrow. She keeps walking, not acknowledging him. I'm still a few steps back. He continues to leer at her, up and down, as she keeps on her way down the mountain. He takes a step, begins to follow her, then I arrive. In a smooth, stealth motion, I take the pistol from its place at the small of my back, between my sweaty skin and khaki cotton shorts. I smash into the bridge of his nose with the butt of the gun, then again into his temple as he leans forward and cups his hands over his face. His friends suck in their laughter and chatter; they stand stunned, staring at the gun. He doubles over, but I pick him up by his shirt. I grab the waist of his pants and rip till the button tumbles to the ground between our feet and the zipper bursts open. I tug his pants down his thighs as blood makes a river down his forearms from where he holds his nose. I put the barrel of the gun to his scrotum and pull the trigger. Ears ringing, drunk with power, splattered with his blood, I release him to crumble at my feet. Turning away, I stride briskly to catch her. She's still walking ahead toward the women swaying up from the city market with baskets of mangoes and rice and beans balanced on their heads. I put my arm around her waist, pull her toward me and we keep walking.

Scene Two. We lie next to each other. Light drains gently around the room from the low-burning kerosene lamp on the table beside the bed. Dogs bark occasionally on the front porch, guarding the perimeter of deep sleep. The clouds, slowly assembling since afternoon, reach critical mass in the darkness and release their pent-up tears, gently at first and then without restraint. I soak in the rhythmic roar, almost sanctifying, on the tin roof. Suddenly the dogs explode with angry, aggressive barks, followed by sudden silence from one and then yelps followed by silence from the other two. Crack! The front door in the next room shudders. I bolt up, she rolls over sleepily and opens her eyes. I scramble naked out of bed, reach the other room and—crack! The single-bolted wood door won't stay closed long. Loud talking starts up outside. My cries for help—"Ahmwhay! Ahmwhay!"—won't carry farther than ten feet in the downpour, and our nearest neighbor lives a hundred feet away. She's sitting up now, looking at me. "Dress!" I scramble to turn up the lamp but knock it over, shattering the room into darkness. There's a flashlight somewhere. Find it! Crack! The rain pounds. Robbers or a mob? Machetes or guns? We hurry into shorts, T-shirts, Tevas. We each have a flashlight. "Follow me." Crack! The door is ready to give. "Now," I say, then open the back door to run across the uncovered, smooth cement of the back patio, then down through the woods toward town. But by my second step my feet are sliding out from under me. Then darkness. I awake, head in blinding pain, rain pellets hammering. I hear faint screams. Grasp for Samson's last, desperate strength. Crawl, soaking, back toward the house. Two flashlights are dancing around. They're wrestling her, screams. I'm pure action, no thought. My left hand takes a machete. I give blows, receive them. Blood. The three of them sprawl groaning across the bed, on the floor. I grab her, a towel, the travel wallet with cash, passports, credit card. We scramble up the hill, falling repeatedly in the mud. I'm sobbing. I turn and shine the light on her face, not sure what I'm looking for. She's expressionless. I pound and scream to convince the neighbor to open his door. He takes us down the muddy mountain road, treacherously, in his battered truck, to the old Holiday Inn in the city. I check in. She sits, wrapped in a towel, on a lobby chair upholstered with tropical flowers. I thank the neighbor, hand him a soggy twenty-dollar bill. We go to our room. She showers for hours, bathroom door locked. I wrap my forearm in gauze and tape supplied by the front desk. I cry sitting on the edge of the bed, pausing to call the American Airlines number in the United States to make a reservation for the 8 a.m. flight, a few hours away now. "Two seats left," the service representative says in a slight Southern drawl, "not together though." I lower my forehead into my hand, start weeping gently again, and say, "Yes, we'll take them."

Q: So . . . why are your anxieties so woven with violence?

A: These are 96 percent fear, 3 percent my mind's attempt to strategize possible defenses and 1 percent fantastical revenge. The scenes storm my psyche, but the details about our home and daily life are accurate. And if I'm going to uncover my fears—and also make it through today and then sleep a little tonight—I need the 1 percent. Though there's little to hold in the second scene. Subtract the revenge, and each scene, including the next one, spirals down closer for a peek at my naked fear. My imagination grasps for the power to respond in kind.

Q: When did these first take root in your imagination?

A: I don't know. Envisioning any of this is repulsive. I hate it. It's not by choice. One semi-comical danger is planting seeds that might blossom into attempting similar action in real life, which would of course go horribly wrong.

Q: Did you have similar thoughts living in the United States? Or when you traveled and lived in other places?

A: The difference is my life is now joined to hers. She's a strong, independent, beautiful woman. She wouldn't say she needs to be protected, but as her husband, aren't I supposed to take some responsibility for that? Haiti can, as people see on CNN, be cruelly violent. But other than cruder tools (machetes, burning), I'm not sure it's culturally more violent than the United States. Because of my citizenship and relative wealth, in one sense I have far more *power* than almost everyone I know and see here. But I don't have the power of guaranteed safety for me—or her. And then there are increasing stories of political violence. Living cross-nationally, cross-racially, cross-culturally, and cross-economically leaves you feeling exposed in ways lots of other people have to live with all the time.

Q: So you haven't felt this way before?

A: When I lived in Albania five years ago, I fantasized about bursting in with a Kalashnikov and mowing down the thugs in a house near mine where I was told they trafficked young girls as prostitutes/slaves, abducted in Russia or Eastern Europe and on their way down to Greece or Italy or the Middle East. I never saw the girls, since they were moved through late at night, but I envisioned them so scared and so young and so broken. Killing men who would do this, even in my dreams, provided the comforting delusion that such protection for the girls existed. In real life I did nothing heroic to save them. When it comes to her, I'm scared I'll have nothing heroic to offer either.

Q: So these aren't the only scenes you've imagined?

A: Right . . .

Scene Three. One afternoon on the tap-tap, as we jerk and swerve through the overcrowded, overheated downtown, there's a fiery political discussion about U.S. involvement in Haitian politics. As usual when politics arise, she and I don't say a word, avoid everyone's eyes, pretend not to understand. A man about twenty-five, dressed in jeans, black clunky loafers and a neatly pressed, brown cotton shirt has been silent too. He dismounts. He turns back, 1960s-like revolver in his hand, shoots her once in the center of the chest. "Noooooo!" I scream as she falls bloodied into my lap. Others scream, scramble off the tap-tap. I follow them off after laying her gently on the pickup's bed. I pursue with long, deliberate strides. He turns, acid smirk. I don't slow. Rage. His gun barrel closer with my every step, aimed between my eyes. My screaming is incomprehensible to me and probably everyone else. Street noise stunned silent; market women stop haggling. An avocado is suspended midair, mid-transaction. Spittle dripping down the corners of my lips. He won't yet pull the trigger. Livid, insane, I keep toward him. Facing me squarely now, he looks back over his shoulder, down the street. I taste blood from when I kissed her wound. Why aren't I with her? I stop and spit in his face. The saliva mixed with blood hangs from the barrel of the cowboy gun. Smells like burn. Inexplicably he hasn't yet pulled the trigger. He wipes away my saliva with the back of his hand. He looks to the merchant women on the side of the street. I attack. The gun falls.

On the chinked asphalt, I gouge into his eyes, I smash his skull again, again, again. His blood sprays up and commingles with hers. I realize, and then stop, nauseous. The gun lies haphazardly to his right. Straddling his body, three times I pull the trigger six inches from his chest.

With numb legs, I stumble back to the tap-tap twenty yards away, keeping the pistol with me should someone get in the way. "Drive! Hospital! Fast! Drive!" I throw the wad of bills from my pocket on the driver's lap as I stagger by and jump into the back. Cradle her into my lap on the blood-soaked bed of the tap-tap. My chest heaves, but not for killing a man. My heart, too, feels fatally wounded, pounding out its last beats. It doesn't matter how fast we drive.

⌒

A: My faith, whatever its strengths or weaknesses, some days seems an inadequate antidote for fear's poison, drip, drip, dripping into my blood all day, through the night.

Q: The way your imagination unfurls here, is this in character for you?

A: I've never owned a gun. My only time firing one was missing a sparrow with a friend's .22 rifle when I was about thirteen. My last fight was in fourth grade; we rolled in the grass and clutched to a draw. I don't remember even once yelling at someone. I've backed down before. Now this all seems inadequate. Feeling so vulnerable triggers a desire to be someone vastly different than I am. Someone more powerful. Someone who could defend myself and kill a powerful man with a single blow. Defend her in any circumstance, from anyone, from anything.

Q: Impotence in the face of life's dangers.

A: Even in my loftiest delusions, my ability to protect is laughable. Look at the first half of Scene Three, when a random man pulls a gun. What could I have done? Or in the scene with the guy leering at her, which is way less serious but happens every week? What will I be able to do in a thousand other realistically possible situations, whether malicious or accidental? Nothing. Nothing. And God is a demonstrably untrustworthy protector too. God's lack of preventive action is seared into the daily news. And since he's not blowing rapists' scrotums off with a .45 or chopping up slave traders with machetes and Kalashnikovs, I grope with my silly Rambo daydreams.

Q: So articulating these scenes somehow helps control your fears?

A: What would you do to rid your world of fears? Men have killed millions in the quest. And they're still killing today. Articulating these fears makes it worse. It's horrific to imagine someone you love in these circumstances before they're actually faced, when they hopefully won't ever be faced. It's an attempt at preemptive—if illusory—control. Maybe these scenes are part of my feeble reach for hope in justice, savage though it may be, which will thus buoy a saving measure of faith in a final accounting and reversal . . . and so in God . . . and so in life.

And so find the courage, in this world, to love her.

Q: Why did you do it this way, with questions and answers and scenes?

A: I couldn't take it on directly. Needed to depersonalize it, make it slightly fictional, make it like I was participating in someone else's questions rather than the thoughts in my own head.

Q: What's the next scene?

A: No. Too far, too much already.

A DROP OF WATER

Eighteen inches above the recently finished concrete floor, which is covered in puddles of water, stands our little wood-frame bed, our ark. Every couple of minutes a drop of condensation falls from the tin roof to land on us. Surrounded by damp clothes, damp walls, damp food and emboldened mold, we shift together in a slow motion dance, gently drifting up, entangled, toward consciousness. The blanket keeps us relatively dry; our bodies keep each other mostly warm in the cool nights of January mountain weather. Farther up the hill cocks crow and a donkey issues an extended, comical bray. For a while we resist but eventually break through the surface of consciousness with a loud *pppshshshshshhSH-SHSHHSH* just outside our window. Shelly whispers into the dawn, "What was that?"

"I think it's Pouchon pouring sand into the pile," I yawn.

"Oh," she says, rolling gently into me for a final cuddle, "and happy birthday!"

Seven days ago we moved into our new home. Yesterday, after we mentioned to Jean Louis our newly poured concrete floor was undryable, he said it could take a month or two *"pou li pap swe,"* "to stop sweating." In this humid rainy season, the tin roof is also sweating. Our new home is effectively a miniature tropical rain forest system. Today I turn thirty-one—hovering, it seems, between liquid and solid, between flood and rainbow.

We have lived in Haiti for one year and ten days, one-third of our marriage. What a fool I feel like, lying here with everything in our house soaking wet while having to put on a whimsical, upbeat display for Shelly. This has been the hardest year of her life, she says unequivocally. Unrelenting intensity and sadness, too much, all around. (Of course, there is joy, too, but surrounded by ubiquitous hardship.) Near the end of the year, Shelly found a term—half joking, half serious—for what she'd been experiencing: *soft torture*. She kept exclaiming "Uncanny!" as she read an *Atlantic Monthly* essay by Mark Bowden that detailed strategies of soft torture: irregular eating, sleep deprivation, a lack of control over one's schedule and life, sudden vacillations between kindness and meanness, temperature extremes, wetness, an unknown future and so on. The year left us slightly battered. This new house is an attempt to find a sustainable way to keep living here. To keep our relationship working. To keep Shelly here.

I regret that everything has been so hard for her—and I'm resentful that it has been. My year was difficult but very good—and better than the previous few. Undeniably, life here is arduous, and more so for most everyone other than us. Yet there are two reasons I find this life more desirable than the most comfortable suburb in all America. First, I'm doing work with Haitian colleagues that I believe is good and siding with people who need more people on their side. Second, there's something about the desperation of life here that resonates with how desperate life itself really, actually, is. On the surface, an American suburb is a place where life is orderly, manicured, manageable. Here, the surface is raw and needy and clawing. There is some reassurance in living where the exterior life, with all its ragged desperation—and glimpses of beauty and faith and spontaneous dancing—resonates more with the interior experience of being human.

Soon a group of men would arrive outside for a morning meeting scheduled to kick-start the final stage of construction, which is still tangled in a thicket of accusations, rumors and delays between the workers and Jean Louis. Apparently this is standard fare, and both sides tell me that eventually things will work out. The front and back porches are not yet cemented, so we track dirt and pebbles into our house each time we enter, and that dirt becomes mud in our swampy interior. The disagreements between various workers can be maddening—and yet with 65 percent of people unemployed and 50 percent malnourished, the possibility of plunging into hunger from losing a job is a palpable, haunting presence. Even minor business interactions are charged with the high stakes of survival. When is the next time Wilio—with fiancée pregnant—will find a job? What if Jean Louis's reputation is tarnished, but he still has to provide for Jezina and their three children in elementary school? Overwhelming. I only know to focus with them on the immediate goal. Any academic disassociation collapsed two months ago: I'm not seeking anthropological insights into my new culture, nor am I fascinated by Haitian approaches to negotiation/money/work/budgets. I just want the house done. On hearing of our decision to build, Haitian colleagues would shake their heads, smile and say, "*Bon kouraj.*" Literally: "Have courage." Figuratively: "You're crazy."

I get out of bed, put on flip-flops, and flip-splosh my way outside to greet Pouchon as he finishes another trip and dumps out the bucket he carries on his head: *pppshshshshshhSHSHSHHSH.* He had walked up the steep, narrow path to our house. He smiles his overbite smile. His face is dusted in a fine layer of sand, as are his disintegrating T-shirt, shabby dress slacks and cheap plastic flipflops.

"*Bonjou,* Pouchon. How are you? It rained last night; isn't the sand too heavy to carry now? Why not wait till later?"

"Oh, *bonjou.* Good to see you. *Pa pi mal*—not too bad. How are you? Yes. Yes, a little heavy. Heavy, but it's got to be done." If Jesus correctly predicted that the meek will inherit the earth, then expect Pouchon to someday have vast holdings spanning rivers and valleys, mountains and plains. If fortunate, I'll get to work in his fields.

~

The meeting seems to go well, and the work on the porches, in addition to Pouchon's carrying sand, will supposedly restart tomorrow, though I've learned to consider even the surest, most straightforward plans with a Zen dispassion provided by an out-of-context quote I saw by the former U.S. ambassador to Haiti (1957–1960), Gerald A. Drew: "In Haiti I believe nothing I hear, and only half of what I see."

Now to embark on our daily trip down to the office—a quadrathalon of sorts.

Stage one: Try not to slip and crack your tailbone on the way down the dirt-and-rock mountain path, which is especially treacherous if rain has fallen the night before. The steep descent takes ten minutes, goes past several homes, past Maxime's rusted-out freezer used to cool Coke bottles (by putting a large block of ice inside), past goats nibbling on grass, women swaying their way up with baskets on their heads and men rhythmically swinging hoes in their fields.

Stage two: Squeeze with a dozen people into the back of a tap-tap and tense your body as you jostle down the dirt road, hoping not to compact any vertebrae. We pass through a small market on either side of the road. Squatting behind a pile of five measly tomatoes and two smallish heads of cabbage is a woman in a blue skirt with a large straw hat protecting her from the sun. Each day dozens of similar scenes are open to Rorschach-like interpretation: Do you see profound, courageous resiliency or a scene that is heartbreakingly pitiful? We arrive in the city, disembark and pay the driver ten gouds (about twenty-five cents).

Stage three: Walk down through Pétionville (the relatively upscale twin to Port-au-Prince). It's the same old universal story of disparity, made especially stark because images of a Hummer driving by and glimpses into the window of a jewelry store selling Rolexes are juxtaposed with cruelly stacked one-room concrete tenements and dirty boys begging. Negotiate the streets past women vendors, past the clinic in front of which a young pregnant woman recently died on the sidewalk because, it was alleged, she was a few dollars short of getting treatment for eclampsia; past the regular boys asking for five gouds or "one dollah" (usually chat a little and give to a few of them). This morning as I negotiate the crowds and dodge tap-taps and speeding SUVs, I hear a man loudly call, "*Psssst! PSSsssst!*" There are other people nearby, but often such calls are directed toward me—maybe to ask for money, to start a conversation or to request help securing a visa to the United States. It's only 9:00 a.m., but I'm not feeling up to this today. Leave me alone. On his third, shrill "*PSSSSSssssssttttt!*" I give in, turn. He's a slight man in attractive, fastidiously pressed clothes. He's doing an awkward come-to-me wave followed by a motion to the cement. It's a new gesture that doesn't obviously translate into either "give to me" or "talk to me." I pause and yell, "Yes, what?" The same mysterious gesture. So I reluctantly start back toward him. Then (did he know it was my birthday?) he yells, "Come back here! Come and get your money!" He points down at a crumpled blue twenty-five goud bill I had dropped. I shake his hand, thank him and walk away laughing because one is never in control here, never sure what's next. I feel guilty for my initial cynicism—in this place that provides endless opportunity for guilt because it's impossible to give enough.

A year into living here, with my messianic adrenaline long ago spent, we try to live simply, find ways to help while doing as little damage as possible and play a tiny role in reversing the damning cycles. Like giving yourself as a raindrop despite not knowing how it might help the garden, or even a single flower, to grow. Certainly saints and conquerors have grander visions of changing the world, but at thirty-one, I'm maturing into (resigning to?) these parameters.

Stage four: Suck in your breath and squeeze into a compact car (this morning, a decrepit four-door Honda Civic) with six other sweaty bodies (three in front, four in back). Jam your hip into the exposed metal of the door, then make the ten-minute dash to the finish line. The ride is downhill, with a few short, flat stretches. Several of the drivers, including this morning's, try to cruise all the way down in neutral with the engine off. I admire their resourcefulness to save a few pennies in gas, even as it causes several decisions—such as swerving around a parked van rather than hitting the brakes—that endanger our lives. Each passenger pays the driver five gouds for the pleasure.

With the commute finished, I arrive at the office and talk with an acquaintance who, along with his young wife, had recently put their baby in an orphanage. Shelly and I would love for Shelly to be pregnant before my next birthday. But how does one bring another child into this world when that little girl—about six months old, with crinkly hair and big brown eyes, whose fist has wrapped around my little finger—is probably crying in a crowded room of cribs a few miles away and definitely not receiving enough touch or care or love? Deep breath.

Moving to my little table, I work on a Creole booklet that explains a method of Bible study based on *lectio divina,* an ancient Christian practice of reading Scripture prayerfully, meditatively and repeatedly, which has been used in some form since the fifth-century Benedictine monks. I have no meetings in or out of the office today; everything is slowing down as people become reluctant to travel amidst the political unrest. As I've worked with Haitian colleagues on different education issues, several of us have come to think this Bible study method would be useful here. The majority of Haitians are Chrisitan, and people's spiritual lives are vibrant—from the Vodou drums keeping rhythm for all-night fetes to grocery store cashiers reading small New Testaments midday on the job—but more than half the adult population is illiterate. Power is often abused, including by some pastors who lord their educational, spiritual and hermeneutical advantage over their congregations. The study method we're promoting values everyone's words and interpretations, including those who can't read. Selfishly, I like that I'll get to spend more time learning about God and the Bible from Haitian sisters and brothers. We hope it will provide a helpful spiritual tool that fosters unity, critical reflection, and shared learning in churches and communities.

This is natural work for me since I have a graduate degree in theology and think churches can and should be locations of liberation for individuals and the community. This fits well with Beyond Borders' wider work with literacy centers, teacher training and children's rights. At the same time, when I survey the health, political, ecological and economic problems crippling this country, I feel slightly ashamed that I can't contribute much more— that I'm not also retooling IMF intervention to structurally improve the financial situation of my neighbors, not reshaping U.S. import policy to quickly create five thousand new jobs, not delivering miraculous peace to this toxic political situation, not offering a doctor's healing touch to save a pregnant woman and her unborn child from eclampsia (that I'm not Dr. Paul Farmer), not implementing ingenious environmental solutions for erosion or for sewage problems in the slums. My contribution here sometimes feels discouragingly meager, but we're helping to get at some of the root problems in education.

Our organization doesn't own shiny Land Cruisers. We ride

public transportation, we spend as much energy on *how* we work as on what we're doing, we earn small salaries (the Haitians and Americans earn the same amount), we have no hierarchy, decision-making power is shared equally among Haitian and American staff, and we live in the communities—not sequestered in bourgeois apartments or compounds. The purpose is to keep us sensitive to people's daily reality, which should then help us offer education and training that helps Haitians build their own better future. So with all these caveats, what a privilege to work closely with these Haitian colleagues. I've seen teachers and schools transformed so children are more deeply valued and teachers gain the confidence to teach rather than just demand memorization. I've seen pastors start to approach leadership and Scripture as opportunities for service and liberation—and take a step away from the temptation to dominate. I've prayed next to illiterate peasant farmers who know God much better than I do and are surprised by and grateful for the chance to share their thoughts with others, who benefit from their wisdom. I've seen market women learn to count, add and read in literacy classes.

While working at the office, I go for a quick walk to find a lunch of fried bread and *pikliz* on the street. When I return, someone in the office has the radio on. The squawking reporters' voices are staccato, fearful, gasping for breath amidst the chanting and screaming and anger. Another demonstration against embattled President Aristide today. In yesterday's protest, a thirteen-year-old boy was killed (along with forty-five others in the political violence by now). I can't understand the reporter's frantic Creole. Shelly came down from our house after me and went straight to a meeting on Rue Delmas. Shelly is out on the street. Why isn't she here with me? Why am I thinking only of her and not also the others who are unquestionably in danger? I stop working to ask a colleague to decipher the breathless chaos. It's further downtown. Nothing on Delmas yet.

Daily we hear stories like this one, told to us recently by a friend: "Yesterday, my two cousins who are students were walking back from an anti-government demonstration. A group of young, pro-Aristide men pulled up in a truck and asked where they were coming from. 'We were visiting friends,' they said. The men responded, 'Liars,' and then pulled out guns and shot them each in the foot, shattering them to pieces. They're in the hospital now."

⌒

Shelly returns to the office safely and hasn't seen any demonstrations. Our simplistic safety strategy is to regularly ask people where the situation is *cho* (hot), then avoid appropriately. Also, on seeing a large crowd, turn and walk quickly in the opposite direction.

We leave the office and head up toward home together, a reverse quadrathalon not always welcome at the end of the day. At the grocery store, the three regular ladies are standing outside selling fruits and vegetables from baskets perched on their heads. (Without refrigeration, we shop daily and buy most of our goods from "market ladies" on the street. Items like bread and cheese we get from a little grocery store.) One of the women is tiny, maybe four feet ten, ninety-five pounds, and usually sells bananas. Another always poses like she's mad, and the muscles at the hinge of her jaw tense as she berates us for not buying three pineapples from her—though her eyes dance mischievously. The third always has sleepy eyes, a soft smile, and a basket full of avocados; she doesn't compete for attention but lingers longer to talk. Yesterday morning when I passed, only the sleepy-eyed avocado seller was here. I asked for her two friends. "They're both married," she laughed, "so they come later because they have to warm their husbands up each morning." Embarrassingly, I can't remember why she doesn't have a husband, a detail lost among too many stories of husbands leaving, being killed by thieves, dying of illness or only making occasional appearances. Though I wish we could help these women more, we buy from them every day. Shelly slips them extra money every so often when they least expect it. We make each other laugh.

Next Shelly and I cram into a tap-tap. A few blocks toward home, we pass Place St. Pierre, a small park of concrete, trees, grass and benches in front of a big Catholic church that has been a recent starting point for some demonstrations. The tap-tap conversation becomes lively when people turn to tomorrow's strike; nobody plans to send their kids down to school because during strikes some schools have been targeted for violence, an easy way to compel parents to comply. Farther up we reach the narrow road where this morning a woman squatted behind her pitiful tomatoes and cabbage. Her little dirt plot is vacant. This stretch often bottlenecks, and we get stuck when five drivers, each from different directions and angles, keep inching forward to try to claim the advantage. For ten minutes we sit jammed, sweating in the back of the pickup—gridlocked in a dusty, physical metaphor for scarcity.

We hike up the path and pause at the rusted freezer, where I'm greeted with an energetic call of *"Patron!"* by Maxime, who after the brief stint working on our house construction has gone back to selling Cokes. Maxime has bits of grass or wicker stuck in his hair because he leaves his stand at times to earn a little money by carrying heavy loads on his head up the mountain for people. We joke for a while, and then I treat myself to an ice-cold Coke.

We arrive home and almost calm the frantic reception by John and Merline's three dogs when Beebee, our teenage neighbor, appears with a rocking chair on his head. The chair is crafted from wood and dried, woven leaves. My mother- and father-in-law gave me birthday money for it. Sweat is pouring down Beebee's face, past his alert eyes and on either side of his bright smile, which reveals front teeth blackening with cavities like crescent moons. Nobody knew how much the chair would cost, so I had given Beebee the equivalent of forty dollars in gouds. He counts back to me about thirty dollars in change. We each try the chair. Perfect. I get him a glass of water. We sit and talk on the balcony.

After Beebee leaves, Shelly and I take our rainwater bucket baths outside next to the latrine, then she generously leaves me, as a birthday treat, to read in my new chair on the porch as she makes pasta with sautéed vegetables in our kitchen consisting of two propane burners on the floor in a corner. Though it's simple and unfinished and wet, we're beginning to enjoy our little house— close to our neighbors yet tranquil. But I still feel ashamed sometimes: because we're surrounded by trees in a denuded country with only 2 percent (and shrinking) forested land, because we don't live in the slums, because I'm not hungry. Yet the birthday table Shelly has arranged for me (a tradition we picked up from our Woshdlo family) is decorated with a card, a pineapple, lollipops, one light blue candle and some peanut butter made by a neighbor in an old spaghetti sauce jar. It reminds me to also be grateful. I'm profoundly glad we're here. In the card, she's generous and encouraging to me.

Without electricity our evenings are short, and after dinner, with the sun now illuminating the other side of the world, there's not much to do: read, write, talk. Sometimes it's boring and lonely. More often the space that opens when myriad options of prefabricated fun are lacking is filled by rich solitude and companionship. Why lose oneself via other kissers kissing and lovers loving and singers singing and marketers manipulating, when our bodies are here together in the quiet light of a kerosene lamp? Shelly's birthday card promised a massage to end the day. I give my body to her in complete trust. Exhausted, satisfied, broken, grateful, longing, uncertain, selfish, loving, older—I drift toward sleep, suspended between the water beaded on the tin roof above and puddled on the cement below.

BUILDING A HOME (PART III)

I signed and sealed the deed, had it witnessed,
and weighed out the silver on the scales.

JEREMIAH 32:10

A week after my birthday Wilio says, *"Kounyea,* Kent." "Now." I take a stick found in the nearby underbrush and draw a heart in the fresh cement of the front corner of the porch. It is deformed and asymmetrical. Wilio laughs and says to try again as he smoothes out my first attempt with his trowel. My second effort passably resembles a heart, so I write in the middle with a stick "Kent + Shelly 2004." Wilio, his assistants Pouchon and Jacques, and I shake hands, and I pour celebratory shots of Barbancourt.

"Look," they say. "You built your wife a house! She'll be happy!" I was eager for Shelly to return home from the office, partly because I wanted to show her that the house was actually almost done and partly to ensure she was safe and thus ease the extra tightness in my stomach.

We've continued to work through a catalog of tensions as we try to finish the house. Threats (as in, "If you give this job to someone other than me . . .") had been issued. An accusation of paying with counterfeit bills has been bandied—though the accuser then went to a Vodou priest, who declared the accused innocent; the spirits revealed the guilty party as someone down in Port-au-Prince. Neighbors are being told Jean Louis is paying for the last stages of the house, not us—which makes us appear as wealthy white cheapskates. Since the project began, the price of a sack of cement has risen from 170 to 210 gouds. We asked for a cheaper, tin-sheet-surrounded latrine but one day come home to find Jean Louis in the middle of building concrete walls around the little hole in the ground. He even added a decorative flourish on the top corners so it looks like a tiny castle. The cost of the house creeps over five thousand dollars; I choose to stop keeping track. We're more than ready for these men to become neighbors we see regularly rather than workers we see constantly. Sorting out back pay continues to be a problem. We call an early-morning meeting. Wilio and his two assistants, Pouchon and Jacques, are asked how much they are owed. Wilio says fourteen days. Jean Louis counts aloud on his fingers to emphatically conclude Wilio could not have possibly worked more than eight. Voices rise. A tenuous peace has Jean Louis counting out gouds for eleven days' work. I only know to focus on the pragmatic: how to get this done as peacefully and quickly as possible.

The problems aren't all resolved smoothly, but within two weeks of drawing the heart in the soft cement, the work is mostly complete, which has allowed Shelly and me to discover a new, rejuvenating peace (solitude at home!) in our daily life—just as the country's political crisis explodes. We're actually spending more time at the house than we want, since occasionally we stay home during a workday when the radio and neighbors advise avoiding the city streets. We still go to the city most days, however.

But how to convey both the tension and the way life continues on? People are more skittish, but if there are no problems in the area, they still pause on the side of the street and pay five gouds for a shoeshine. Babies are born. We go to work. Everyone who has a job goes to work. Women sell vegetables in the market; other women buy. Then the woman who buys goes home with her vegetables. Her family is relieved when she arrives home safely, with a small plastic sack of tomatoes, onions, chives and eggplant. Then she cooks dinner.

Political demonstrations regularly turn into violent clashes. Students are being beaten, sometimes shot. The state university downtown has been a center point of the anti-government movement. The university's dean was severely beaten, both his knees shattered by pro-government partisans. Daily tap-tap conversations used to be about rain-caused landslides in October. Now they're about how to avoid being caught in the political landslides. Provoked by the murder of their leader, Métayer, the gang in Gonaïves now led by Métayer's brother Buteur has taken advantage of the president's weakness and started grabbing for power in the north of the country. They've been joined by ex–Haitian military (Aristide had disbanded the military in 1994) and other discontents, some of whom are unsavory characters with records of severe human rights abuses who had been living in the Dominican Republic with support, some say, from Haitians abroad and even from some in the U.S. government.

We're aching for the country, and the Jeremiah parallel has become almost comically sad. We build our house as the city crumbles. A kind of siege closes in. The possibility of civil war looms. Five weeks after our new home is (relatively) complete, we're facing the decision of whether or not to stay and live in it.

WILLING TO DIE?

A decision needed to be made. Airports were expected to close any day, and the situation in the city was rapidly deteriorating into violent chaos. With the lights of Port-au-Prince down below, I sat on our porch vacillating. I felt fear and a strong urge toward self-protection, but I also wanted to be vulnerable to love's persuasive power. If my wife were Haitian and didn't have a visa to exit the country, the choice to stay would have been clear and easy.

I kept remembering a German professor in his seventies who told us he wished he had refused to fire his rifle at a target as part of a Third Reich training program. He felt he had implicitly endorsed the Nazis by participating, though he had never fought, had never done anything but train. Recalling the scene half a century later, he said in a hushed, cracking voice, "If I hadn't fired the rifle, I would have been shot and killed on the spot. I've wished for fifty years that I had refused to fire."

I didn't want to be haunted by regrets. I still regretted not doing more for Vera in Albania. I wanted to work on behalf of people who have almost no one on their side. I believed I was on the right team. But I wasn't prepared for a civil war that had no clear, righteous side to support. I wanted to be ready to die in the stand for justice, but as the situation degenerated, I didn't see a cause for which I was willing to give myself. I wanted to be willing to die for the love of my neighbor—but figure (vainly?) my death had better produce *results*.

I was in Haiti because I thought I could help, if in a minor way, and I'd willingly accepted the risks of dangerous public transportation, inadequate health care and crime. But in Port-au-Prince, work of any kind had been suspended; the city was indefinitely on hold. I was helping nobody.

The question of whether to stay in Haiti "in solidarity" remained. Solidarity makes it possible to help more effectively and also serves as testimony both to our neighbors ("We are on your side") and to wider society ("We must not ignore this; we must find a better way"). Extreme acts of solidarity serve as beacons for the rest of us. I'm awed by the moral purity of self-sacrifice, but I'm also repulsed if it seems unnecessary. What good does it do? Maybe sometimes, however, we need to make dangerous, unpragmatic decisions for the good of our neighbors and society. My pragmatism seemed more like selfishness when we considered, through various conversations with neighbors, what our decision would communicate to them: yet another marker of society's breakdown that should be escaped if possible, but that they'd have to endure.

Maybe it would be good to work out a personal cost-benefit formula, a sort of moral calculus to which hard figures could then be applied in situations like this. As I weighed potential costs and benefits of staying in Haiti, I could only come up with:

1. Love of family: leave.
2. Love of justice as an idea: stay.
3. Love of justice in messy reality: leave.
4. Productive love of neighbor: leave.
5. Love of neighbor through solidarity: stay.

But I needed something more scientific. For example, what would be the precise moral calculation of the decision to jump into a raging river to save someone from drowning, given a reasonable but not certain chance I would drown? I would jump into the river to try to save a seven-year-old girl. Maybe I would jump in to save a young single parent, since Shelly would still be there for my children (if we were to have them). No, I wouldn't jump in to try to save a forty-six-year-old bachelor just out on parole after a rape conviction. Yes, I would fight and die to defend my community if a ruthless enemy invaded it. Maybe I would go to the front lines of a UN-sanctioned war to prevent genocide if I could clearly help. No, I would not die to preemptively eliminate a nebulously defined faraway threat. Yes, I would denounce the church hierarchy and structure. Maybe I would step on a Bible. No, I wouldn't blaspheme Jesus. Maybe this exercise would strengthen my courage for future decisions. Maybe not.

༺

On Tuesday, February 24, five days before President Aristide was whisked out of power and two days before the Port-au-Prince airport closed, Shelly and I boarded American Airlines flight 1908 to Miami. The ride to the airport in the back of a pickup was tense. The streets were tranquil, with much less traffic than normal.

"Leave your house only if necessary" was the unassailable wisdom. Did an angry roadblock await around the next bend? We arrived at the airport safely. Took our seats. Felt the plane accelerate and lift off. Coke and pretzels? Yes, please.

As the shacks and denuded brown mountaintops receded below, my hunched shoulders dropped two inches, muscles that had been clenched for weeks released, and a slight headache drifted in. We had decided to leave rather than risk staying in the political chaos down below, which made my stomach nauseous. I ultimately rejected staying because I couldn't see what I would be able to accomplish that would outweigh the risk. We were escaping—leaving behind friends, colleagues and neighbors for whom leaving was not an option. Now it was time to live with the decision.

After leaving Haiti, we stayed for a month with friends in south Florida, working for Beyond Borders on administration, reports, budgets, translation—and following the news from Port-au-Prince on TV and online. The conflict climaxed with the February 29 departure of President Aristide, followed by several days of lawlessness before the U.S. Marines arrived in force. During our first few days back in the States, Haiti shared the front pages with the theatrical release of *The Passion of the Christ*. Men with guns cruised in pickup trucks through Port-au-Prince, preening for the TV news cameras. This image was quickly followed by clips of James Caviezel as the soon-to-be-crucified Christ grimacing amidst gallons of blood. Aristide, former priest and now former president, was sometimes accused of posing as a messiah, and soon after his departure he began decrying the subversive plots of the United States and its allies. Meanwhile, Mel Gibson was decrying the subversive plots against his movie. In light of these scenes, any impulse for self-flagellation over my decision to leave seemed laughable.

While in Florida I found a July 2003 issue of *Outside* magazine
in the "ten-cents bin" at the local library. In it, journalist Peter
Maass recounted his experience reporting on the recent invasion
of Iraq. He and his colleagues drove rented SUVs in a caravan
alongside American Humvees and tanks. He opens the article: "I
do not know the value of life. In every war zone that I find myself
in, I routinely fail to establish a sensible line beyond which I will
not take risks." After spending his first night alongside the soldiers, he saw that this war, like all others, was chaotic and deadly.
"At dawn," he writes, "there was only one direction to go: [onward
with the invasion] . . . the road back to Kuwait was a professional
dead end. I told myself I would stay with this war for now, see
what happened, and pull out if that became the wise thing to do.
Oddly, going deeper into the war was the easy way. Deciding that
the risks were too high and living with the second-guessing and
feelings of cowardice that might afflict me if I retreated and my
colleagues continued on—that would have required real courage."
I felt both rebuked and justified as I sat reading this on a comfortable couch in an air-conditioned room.

As the days went by, Shelly and I received word that everyone
we knew in Haiti was well, though general insecurity prevailed:
carjackings were frequent, and one American woman, a friend of
a friend, was robbed in her home by a half-dozen armed men,
though she and her child were left unharmed. Hundreds had lost
their lives, but an outright civil war had been averted. Meanwhile,
still in Florida, we confirmed our flights to go back. Not long after
that the CNN.com home page led with close-up photos of four
American Southern Baptist missionaries who were shot and killed
while working on a water-purification project in Iraq.

Will there be any hostility on our return to Haiti? Certainly not
from everyone, but perhaps from a small, dangerous minority.
What are we going back to? We're as white and American as the
recently landed Marines, who seemed to be met with indifference

and some resentment. A strongly worded State Department travel warning remains in place. How will the gangs respond? Will kidnappings of foreigners begin in earnest as other sources of revenue dry up? Am I being paranoid? Is living in Haiti during the current political turmoil more or less dangerous than, say, living in a rough neighborhood of Chicago or working as a timber cutter or fisherman—America's two most dangerous jobs?

I'm slightly sick to my stomach again, but this time for going toward what I believe rather than away from it. My faith should gird me up in moments like this. Shelly and I aren't talking much about the decision; we're moving forward simply because returning seems right to both of us. I tried to dissuade her from coming, but she has her own decisions to make about life and death and love. We don't talk about the possibility of dying or of losing each other. This silence seems yet another cowardly failure to me. But I keep searching for courage, for what is right.

We're back sitting next to each other on the airplane. The island's parched landscape is coming into view. I feel the clunk and hear the landing gear lowering as I look down on single-room, concrete-block homes below with the farmers out beside them trying to coax life from their dry, begrudging fields. Time to land again.

5

Revelations

SEEING A LITTLE MORE CLEARLY

It's no secret that making a difference by helping others, in ways small or significant, also makes a difference in us. Generosity, suffering and love burrow deeper into the bones. I think I'm starting to see a little more clearly. New questions keep replacing the old ones. Surfaces give way to more depth.

Vulnerability to need, truth, guilt and failure has also been exposure to joy: the joy of discovery and rebirth, the joy of connection and meaning, the joy of watching some of my idols crash to the ground so there's a better view of God, the joy of falling (a terrifying fall) into God's gracious love because nothing else is enough, the joy of following Jesus while also embracing the indignant faith that shoots through the Psalms.

When we moved into our new house, one of the ways Shelly and I embraced the new, occasional solitude was by reading a psalm together after dinner each night. We've continued after returning to Haiti. The country is relatively stable, but still with intense undercurrents and destabilizing problems. We're glad we're back. The psalmists' darker moments scattered throughout the collection grab our attention:

Nations are in uproar, kingdoms fail;
    he lifts his voice, the earth melts. (46:6)
For I know my transgressions,
    and my sin is always before me. (51:3)

Be merciful to me, O Lord, for I am in distress;
    my eyes grow weak with sorrow,
    my soul and my body with grief. (31:9)

But I am a worm and not a man. (22:6)

Well, the last one is a bit extreme, but it relates to what I've been thinking about lately, which seems to be in the tradition of the Psalms' shadows:

Nothing that I have do I deserve. None of it.

Saying this isn't pious self-flagellation, holier and more dedicated than thou; it's just a fact I can't hide from here. Neither you nor I deserve a single thing we have. I don't deserve my job. I don't deserve a vacation. I don't deserve my beautiful wife or my family or friends. I don't deserve a raise. I don't deserve a comfortable retirement one day. I don't deserve this little house on the mountainside. I don't deserve opportunities. I don't deserve well-fitting shoes. I don't deserve my next meal. I don't deserve for anyone to treat me with respect.

I deserve nothing, except in the abstract way every single girl and boy, woman and man, deserves everything. This isn't a quick disclaimer before rushing through to embrace as rightfully mine everything I do have or to set the stage for the power of positive thinking (which doesn't have any power if you don't have any power).

I don't consider everything I've had to be blessings meted out personally to me by my Creator—as though all the scarcity is thus evidence that the Creator is personally *not* meting out to other people—though I also thank my Creator as the source of everything good that I'll ever have. This seems true and also seems to help me see a little more clearly, like a lens that corrects some of the myopia of selfishness. It sounds negative but feels a little like freedom that leads me to pray . . .

God, our Father and Mother; Christ, my Savior and brother; Spirit, hidden Presence:

I love you because you know and love me. But I know so little of you, glimpses through Christ and mixed messages through the world.

I don't know if I hold you at a distance, or if it's you who hold yourself at a distance from me. I need your intimacy, and yet everything I experience keeps you a mystery.

I'm grateful to you beyond measure, my Creator, my every breath, my grace and mercy. I don't know how to worship you any more than this—with my proud and deceitful and broken heart.

I give you myself—a pittance, but all I have. All I ask is everything. All I ask is you in return.

Christ, I find hope and forgiveness in you—or if I won't, I'm doomed. Forgive me for my selfishness and hypocrisy, for my lust after so much that isn't love, for so many hours and years and opportunities that I piddle away, these gifts I'm supposed to cherish and share. Lead us. Forgive us. Maybe we're supposed to trust you, but you shouldn't have trusted us. How can it be worth it, God?

In you, Christ, I find my light, though it's awfully dark.

I pray for my sisters and brothers who are hurting unbearably tonight—that you would suffer with them, that you would stop their suffering, though I know you won't stop it all or even very much right now. It's more faith than I can muster, yet there's something in me that trusts you—or wants to so desperately that it resembles trust—despite it all, in the midst of it all, because of it all. I call out for you in rage and desperation and hope and doubt and tender love.

Call back to me, I ask. Call us out of our graves, like Lazarus. Weep a tear for us all again, and let us weep with you. Let's all weep together for this beauty and this mess. Then come, Lord Jesus, come and save us somehow, anyhow. And meanwhile show us how to save each other . . .

SKETCHES OF SCARCITY

SCARCITY OF BIRTH CERTIFICATES

President Aristide has been gone for seven weeks, removed by a variety of complex and simple, hidden and exploding reasons—including that he governed in a nation swirling in a cycle of ravaging scarcity. But politics aren't discussed much as seven of us sit in the village of Woshdlo talking on Good Friday under the shade of a towering mango tree. Occasionally a dense, green *fransik* mango lands a few feet away with a deep thud, but nobody wants to move out of the shade. Shelly and I came from Port-au-Prince to spend the holiday weekend with our Woshdlo family. Frefre (the neighbor whose cow dragged me through the field) is trying to flirt a woman into being his third or fourth *madam;* the count is constantly in flux. His foot is infected, so he's been walking with a slight limp, but he still radiates an intense vitality earned by farming his plots of plantain, bean, corn and okra fields by hand, hoe and machete. "I'm too old for you," the woman teases. "Not true," he objects. Round they go, his arm, flecked white from vitiligo's loss of skin pigmentation, wrapped around her as she playfully pushes him away. People are prodding him: "What can you say to her 'too old' defense? You don't even know how old you are!" Mid to late thirties would be a good guess; he has an eighteen-year-old son. Unembarrassed, he says, "When I was young, everyone just called me *tigason* [little boy]. I never knew when I was born. Once when a school principal asked me how old I was, I just said, '*Tigason*.'" Everyone laughs. "But the principal wasn't impressed. He kicked me out of the class and beat me with a stick." Since he can't prove he's older by birth date, a new method is needed. He shows a few gray hairs on his head, but she has some too. "Okay. You want proof? Undeniable proof? No-way-to-refute, ace-in-the-hole, gotta-be-my-woman proof? Then beware women and children," he says as he hikes up his ragged shorts to show a couple of gray pubic hairs (keeping everything else covered). Everyone bursts out laughing, but he's playing it straight and serious. He stays exposed, pointing at the gray hair. "See, I'm older," he says triumphantly. "You can be my *madam!*" Then he invites her to match this proof positive. She changes the subject. People chuckle. He pulls his shorts leg back down and resumes flirting.

~

SCARCITY OF POCKET MONEY ON THE MORNING COMMUTE

To the first boy: "Hi. Haven't seen you in a while. How are you? Here you go."

To the newspaper vendor, waving today's edition frantically: "No, sir. Sorry. Don't read French well. Have a good day."

To the little girl and her sister, who have latched firmly onto both hands: "Okay. Share this. Do you like deep fried bread or plantains better?"

To the second boy, whose hands are thick with the soot of charcoal he'd just been carrying for someone: "Did I give you something yesterday? No? Okay, here."

To the old man with saucer-sized eyeglasses askew, missing one leg, as he hops hurriedly over on crutches: "Sorry, sir. Not today. Pockets are empty."

To the twenty-five-year-old neighbor you see in town who is asking for a job and, if not that, then a hundred gouds: "I'm sorry. I'd love to find you a job, but I honestly don't know of any possibilities."

To the banana vendor, squatting by the side of the road under a wide-brimmed straw hat: "Oh, they look good, *madam!* I'll buy a few on the way back up. *Bòn joune.* See you this afternoon."

To the angry young man demanding I pay his bus fare: "No, I'm not paying for you." (Unspoken: "Why would I pay for someone I've never met before who so obviously hates me?")

To the third boy, with four friends: "Sorry, guys. Not right now."
(To avoid causing a scene, it seems best to give to one or two at a
time.)

～

SCARCITY OF SAFETY

The mother of four and grandmother of two sweats under the shade
of her straw hat. She and her friends are sitting along the busy sidewalk, selling their wares and sharing a snack of avocado and bread.
Midafternoon, they're not selling as aggressively—"Three mangoes
for thirty gouds!" "Come buy some corn!"—as they were earlier
this morning. She left her home up on the mountain about 4:00
a.m., after making coffee for her husband. Cars and pedestrians
and trucks speed past all day; a pungent mixture of sounds and
smells, of gasoline and exhaust fumes and yelling and urine and
blaring horns assaults her senses. She has a large wicker basket of
limes and ten neat little pyramids (six or seven limes in each) on a
plastic bag beside the basket. Five gouds per pile. She doesn't notice
when the yelling gets more intense just up the street, when the
horn blasts a little longer, until the huge white truck catches the
corner of her eye as it barrels onto the sidewalk and slams into her
and her friends. A perfectly round lime escapes her pile undamaged
and rolls down the street, skittering along over pebbles and through
puddles, eventually plunging into a jagged, muddy pothole.

Was that how it had happened? This afternoon on our way home
from work up through the city (stage three of the quadrathalon
commute), Shelly and I passed through an animated crowd. Police
stood around with machine guns at the congested intersection
where the busy Rue Delmas ends. Off to one side is a charred gas
station that was torched in the chaotic days of President Aristide's
departure from power. A large Mack truck was up on the narrow
sidewalk between the gas station and the cars, trucks and pedestri-

ans—where the market women usually sell their cabbages and tomatoes and mangoes and beans. No bodies were laid out, but there was the squashed and scattered debris of tomatoes, limes, carrots, baskets. Depending on who you ask, the truck either lost control or had brake failure. "Many women died" was the word on the street. We buy from women farther up the road so probably don't know any of the women who were struck. The police were there to stop reprisal killings and vengeance burning of the guilty truck.

Just another day here. Again and again till you think more can't be possible. Then again. Boiling water scorches the skin off the upper leg and butt of a neighbor boy in a cooking accident. Part of his body looks like a burnt hot dog. It happens all the time. Last week about two thousand on the island died in flash floods and mudslides.

In another land, kids are bicycling in pristine neighborhood parks with helmets and kneepads and training wheels—how about being able to safely sell the fruits and vegetables from your garden on the street without a huge truck slamming into you? The truck's brakes had probably been bad for ages, with an owner who was squeezing out their final miles of utility. Cutting corners. Couldn't afford a real repair. Save a few gouds. Safety belts? People pile onto the roofs of cargo trucks, pay twelve cents for a long highway trip, then hold on for dear life. Shelly and I once rode for three hours holding on to ropes on top of an ice truck going fifty miles an hour. Vehicle safety inspections? The vehicle is streetworthy if it can move on the street. Water? Hope that your source is semi-potable and only causes occasional diarrhea. Food? Hope that you have enough. Building codes? Build where possible, whatever you can afford, and pray that the floods or earthquakes or mudslides or the Big Bad Wolf doesn't blow it all down, with you inside.

SCARCITY OF EDUCATION

I'm chatting with Maxime next to his rusted-out, horizontal freezer one Saturday afternoon. Just bought a half-liter glass bottle of Coke that is dripping wet from its morning in a pool of melted ice. A man comes up, asks Maxime if he is selling to the *blan*. We start talking. He is probably in his fifties, still clinging to a few yellowish teeth. Warm smile. He wears a black and red "D.A.R.E. to Resist Drugs and Violence" baseball cap. His tight Burberry plaid pants that taper to his ankles appear to have been owned by an American woman in a previous life, before being discarded at the thrift store. As per custom, early in the conversation I ask about his kids. "I have five—three boys and two girls," he says. "Sent them all to school. But me, I'm stupid. I never went to school. My mom died when I was little, so I grew up with my godmother. They treated me like a *ti kouchon,* a little pig. I did all the awful jobs. They didn't send me to school. Didn't want me to learn to read and write. Then I might be able to take advantage of them, like maybe switch their land ownership papers to my name. Like a *little pig.*" He says this with only a tinge of bitterness. It's a normal chat on a Saturday afternoon standing beside the rusted-out freezer. I take a sip of Coke.

~

SCARCITY OF PRIDE

Six months before moving to Haiti, I had met the director of the Haitian branch of a large international charity at a restaurant in northern New Jersey. His charity is the kind that puts your conscience in a blender with their TV commercials of big, sad, innocent, brown eyes pleading for your 1-800 donation. We had talked on the phone and e-mailed each other several times. I liked him. We were to discuss the possibility of my working for him in Haiti (before I decided to come with Beyond Borders). He suggested we meet at Red Lobster. I arrived on time at 12:30 p.m. Go ahead and order first, he said. I purposely chose one of the cheapest entrées, something like sautéed shrimp over angel hair for $11.99. Then he coolly ordered a fish dip appetizer for about $3.50. That's all. Slightly embarrassed and plenty annoyed at the way he seemed to set me up, I worked my way through the mountain of pasta as we discussed helping people in the third hungriest country in the world.

More than a year after the shrimp lunch, after I'd been in Haiti for five months, Shelly and I arranged to meet him at his office. He was interested in our organization, and we were interested in learning more about his work. Despite the Red Lobster maneuver, I still liked him and looked forward to seeing him. I was sick again with my recurring intestinal problem, but at that time we seldom left Woshdlo to come to the capital, so I didn't want to cancel. Gurgling in the morning, my stomach was now rumbling and grumbling. We arrive at a huge building. Rows of brand-new, white SUVs. Multi-million-dollar operation. Sit down in the first-floor waiting room. Offered coffee, I refuse with a hand over my stomach and sweat beading on my forehead. "You don't look well," Shelly says. "I'll make it," I mutter and ask the receptionist for the bathroom. Ten minutes later I stagger out reluctantly: the toilet wouldn't flush. I'm a little dizzy. Back to the waiting room till Mr. Director sends his assistant down to give us a tour. On the second floor, the assistant says, "This is the head of our agriculture program." Then, in a room with a long table piled with boxes of letters, and five workers huddled over them sorting and translating, the assistant says, "Here's where we process letters from child sponsors." I say: "Um, nearest bathroom, please?" Just down the hall. Please no, this won't flush either. Alas, sneak out and away. I find the assistant and Shelly as I overhear a cluster of employees talking about a generator/water problem. Go up to the third floor to see the director. Good to see him. Talk for a while and then, according to Shelly's later account, I turn pale and drift into a nonsensical monologue . . . until I quickly stand and ask where the nearest toilet is. He points me to a nearby fancier executive bathroom. Cramping, exploding, disgusting . . . and no flush. Slump back to his office, mustering just enough strength not to fall—and to feel humiliated. Goodbye.

Got a ride back to where we were staying—where I vomited, continued with the diarrhea and for the first time broke out in a severe case of could-make-you-lose-your-mind, bodywide hives. Cheap tricks in Red Lobster were unnecessary. His country's water took care of humbling me quite effortlessly.

~

SCARCITY OF MEDICAL EXPERTISE

Limes kill all germs and bacteria. Women are to blame for infertility because the baby is implanted by the man as a fully viable embryo and the woman needs only provide "good soil." Coconut milk and beer will cure your diarrhea, which is certainly the result of heat/water/food/dust (choose one). Sprite will cure your diarrhea. Coke will fix your upset stomach. Put a single lime in your water pitcher, then the water is fine. Tea made with this leaf will cure your diarrhea. No, that one will make it worse, but this one will help. Never let a pregnant woman drink that tea. If vitamins don't take the (malarial?) fever of the little girl away, then the Vodou priest's potion can. As a swollen, puss-filled, obviously infected, strangely colored cut on your thumb threatens to turn gangrenous, the doctor at one of the country's better hospitals prescribes an anti-inflammatory for arthritis—and that's all. People assert their medical opinions to strangers during chance meetings on public transportation with more confidence than a world-renowned M.D. at a World Health Organization conference. Declarative medical solutions are on the loose, not sequestered to the hallowed corridors of white lab coats. I've tried some of the various remedies; maybe they helped. And though it's ultimately to the experts I turn when experiencing threatening intestinal problems, a crisp, cold lager mixed with fresh, sweet coconut milk sounds surprisingly appealing.

◦—

SCARCITY OF TECHNOLOGY

Women and children ceaselessly carry water by the gallons on their heads up and down the steep mountain path. A teenage boy pulls grass by hand for several hours to provide his cow a single meal. A woman sits sweating for three hours stoking a hot charcoal fire to boil a pot of rice to feed a family of thirteen (and whoever else drops by). A hundred feet inland from the sea, boys dig crabs out of the sand to sell—with fingers scarred from the vigorous defenses of crab claws against the hands invading their dark, three-foot-deep holes. A barefoot man pushes a wheelbarrow with more than a hundred pounds of plantains up the steep, busy, asphalt road. Seven men in a staggered row swing their hoes in unison as they turn the stubborn earth into small rows of hills and valleys to receive seeds of corn. The next day one of the men returns to throw three corn kernels in each newly dug hole, as his three sons (aged five, seven and ten) trail behind him kicking dirt over the seeds and gently patting it down with their bare feet so chickens won't come and rob them of their precious harvest before it starts growing. A man sits all day in the dry riverbed—every day, every day but Sunday—a hammer in his hand, hand-me-down junior-high lab goggles on his eyes, every day, sitting on a pile of rocks in the sun, hammering softball-sized rocks into grape-sized rocks, every day, swing after swing after swing, big piece into littler piece into little piece, all day, every day, breaking down rocks for use in the construction of someone else's house. And he smiles and says hi across the blindingly white rocks as the sun glares down.

❧

SCARCITY OF POSSIBILITIES

When he arrives, the sun is fading to a faint mustard stain in the sky. Birds might let out a staccato chirp or two, but they don't sing. They might fly from this branch to that, but no frivolous swoops or soars. He's bright and articulate, about twenty-five and a high-school graduate (a relative rarity). With no energy for initial small talk, he asks for the seventh time in three months, less as inquiry and more as dirge, "So what do you know about scholarships for studying in the States? Any ideas about getting a student visa?" His sad sweetness has the aroma of over-fermented wine. He never asks directly, probably because a direct answer would be devastating—the well gone permanently dry, cactus and rattlesnake taking over a lush tropical isle. As we talk, a lizard camouflaged against the rough, creviced bark of an avocado tree does spastic push-ups—up-down, up-down. Maybe a small bug will wander by and offer itself as a meal. Maybe not. Prospects for a job or for a student visa (if you're without wealth or significant connections) are just slightly more likely than an avocado tree producing coconuts. We finish talking, and my eyes feel like they've been saturated by his personal cloud, ready to unleash a thousand years of rainfalling, rainfalling, rainfalling, rainfalling tears.

❧

SCARCITY OF POSSIBILITIES (PART II)

Two-thirds of Haitians would leave immediately for the States if given the chance, says one poll I read, which, not surprisingly, corresponds with the formal unemployment rate. About a million Haitians live in the United States. Sandra, our neighbor in Woshdlo until she moved to live with family a fifteen-minute walk away after her husband beat her, is immeasurably proud of her twenty-three-year-old son who made it *lòt bò dlo* ("to the other side of the water"). She's been telling us about him for weeks. A small town in Florida. Do you know it? He sends me money every month. He just got in a minor car accident, but he's okay. He works so hard. So proud of him. He has a great job. He wears a uniform. Every month he sends money back. Wouldn't be able to eat without his help. Sandra hands us the photo, then steps back to relish the moment. He stands spiffy and smiling next to the cash register in his Chick-fil-A visor and polo shirt. He contributes to the approximately one billion dollars sent annually from the Haitian diaspora to support this anemic economy. Looking at the photo, I feel a surge of unrestrained pride too.

SCARCITY OF RAINBOWS

About two thousand people died in May 2004 during heavy flooding and mudslides near the Haiti-Dominican border. A friend's family lives in that area. His mom, who was in Port-au-Prince visiting at the time, lost her gardens, her cows, goats, pigs and horse. His cousin and cousin's wife died. As the floodwaters rose, the two adults had carried two of their four children, seven and ten years old, to safety. When they waded back into the rushing, rising water to cross and rescue their other two younger children, the parents were swept away. The water kept rising and eventually took their house and the two kids who were still awaiting rescue. The seven- and ten-year-old stood watching in the distance on dry ground—uncertain how to interpret God's rainbow promise to never again destroy the world by water.

SCARCITY OF MERCY

God, do you see the way his skin is being burned—literally, daily, scorched and tightened, pinkish with black, charred scabs up and down his arms and legs, across his face? An albino, left naked to the sun by his own skin. Why would you place one of your children here, so defenseless without pigmentation—just under the Tropic of Cancer and, at age eighteen, probably on his way to early death by cancer itself? Why let his mother and father fall in love? Or let their recessive albinism genes take effect in their child? You've overheard the conversations when people seem to be fiercely proud and also seem to hate the color of their own skin. You've heard them say, "My hair's ugly. Your hair is so pretty, smooth, long. My hair isn't smooth. It's African." And you've seen the hateful expressions toward white skin for its association with slavery and robbery and torture. And so your little pan-seared son lives unprotected on a farm plain in a one-room, tin-roofed house as a miraculous incarnation—100 percent descendant of slaves, 100 percent target of self-loathing, 100 percent representative of the oppressor. And now what miracle to request of you, God? That one day this black man will actually wake up black? You hear the children mocking him daily. You see the way he hangs his head when he walks outside his yard, though he is sweet and smiling in the confines of his house. You see how it's a grace to receive his warmth, but bittersweet because it comes partly because we receive the same taunts as we walk through the field together, even though so little about our lives is similar. "Look , two *blan!*" Your bright tropical sun gives life to the sugar cane and beans and cornstalks all around, as that same sunlight rips into your child's raw, tender skin. *Lord, have mercy. Christ, have mercy. Lord, have mercy.*

⌒

SCARCITY OF STABILITY

Haiti's ancestors were imported to the island as slaves. They fought for and won their independence from France on January 1, 1804. Since then . . .

New constitutions: 1804, 1805, 1806, 1807, 1811, 1816, 1843, 1849, 1874, 1879, 1889, 1902, 1918, 1932, 1935, 1946, 1950, 1957, 1964, 1971, 1983, March 10, 1987 (current).

American and UN occupations and/or peacekeeping: 1915–1934; 1994–1995; March 2004–present.

Coups d'etat/assassinations/overthrows: More than thirty. Precise definition is difficult, as illustrated by the forced ouster/resignation-under-pressure of President Jean-Bertrand Aristide on February 29, 2004.

～

SCARCITY OF TRUTH

Would you tell the truth if each political regime-change tossed up waves of revenge (called *dechoukaj,* or "uprooting") that were manifested in vigilante executions or the dramatic burning of homes and people? Would you say, "Yes, George is home," when you don't know who is asking for George, or why? Would you tell people your name and where you live—when maybe they're asking because they're friendly or maybe because they're in desperate situations, ready and willing to do desperate things? If you needed money for food or for your children's shoes and tuition, would you hesitate to plead for money for "my extremely sick child," a story that might increase your chance of eliciting a donation? Would you make up stories about the churches and orphanages you may or may not run so that you could tap into the stream of American charity dollars flowing down to your island—and so help your family and the consciences of the foreigners, if not any orphans or parishioners? Would you tell the truth? If so, would you survive?

SCARCITY OF CONTROLS

Special treat: Shelly and I went out one afternoon for pizza in a cozy, wood-paneled restaurant. At the table next to ours sat an adult foreigner and a wiry, ten-year-old Haitian boy dressed in jeans and a red-and-blue-striped polo shirt. Rumor has it that this foreigner's charity is a cover for sexual abuse. The accusations come from normally trustworthy sources, but truth is slippery here. There's that version, then there's the opposing claim that saintly work is being maligned. Stories like these circulate about some orphanages and different ministries. And what regulation, protection, control is there for the kids—some of whom are swept up to have their lives saved, others of whom are swept into abuse? Meanwhile, distant do-gooders send their money thinking it's going to rescue the poor, vulnerable children of Haiti. Sometimes it does, sometimes the opposite. I try to imagine positive reasons why this tender boy, sitting so carefully in his chair, merited dinner at a nice restaurant.

SCARCITY OF GREED

Paint in short, bold strokes a picture of a family sitting around in their yard under the shade of a tree and passing around tin plates of white rice with black-bean sauce. They're all somewhat malnourished, including the scrawny dog with clumps of fur fallen out, who occasionally has demonic attacks of scratching, moaning and rolling on its back (worms, apparently). The adults never finish their food, but give a couple of spoonfuls to the dog and then give the remaining quarter of the food to the kids. Leave the picture hanging there . . . the image can hint at how they're only getting the world's table scraps. Then the little boy, six years old, who never wears pants (not because he doesn't own a pair, but because he doesn't like pants and this way it's easier to pause for a quick pee on the dirt path) hears you say you're looking forward to eating some mangoes. He slips away, then returns forty-five minutes later with four mangoes he found in a neighbor's field. He's so happy to give them to you. Picture how five or six houses (about seventy people) share a *gòl,* a long stick with a wishbone end used to harvest oranges and mangoes and breadfruit; it's unclear who owns it. Same with the old truck axle in the *lakou,* where all the men come to bang sharpness back into their hoes.

Those who own next to nothing share with others who own nothing. They're not just victims to be idealized, either for good or for bad—good people, bad people, like anyone else, but in extreme circumstances. Subtly evoke echoes of Jesus' Sermon on the Mount. Introduce the complications . . . the demands of sharing pressed on those who have a little something? Talk of how a Haitian we know sometimes hides his car in a carport, doesn't leave it out by the street because everyone will know he's home and many people will come by to ask for help, ask him to pony up in the spirit of communal giving because he has a job. Or just end it with the positive examples, since there is so much beauty here even if it coexists with ravenous scarcity? Find a positive way to conclude. There's so much pain and laughter, hardship and goodness. Let scarcity and abundance, despair and hope, battle it out.

EASTER VIGIL

Maundy Thursday and Good Friday we slept for a combined total of five hours at our Woshdlo family's home. The rat problem has worsened since we left, and I haven't become any more at ease with their company. After little sleep the first night, I asked the eight-year-old boy about their cat. "Oh, the cat died," he said with his regular gleam of mischief. "Now the house is pretty much for the rats. Didn't you hear them last night? It's like they're playing soccer up in the rafters."

We left Woshdlo on Saturday afternoon and cramped and jostled through six hours of public transportation (six different vehicles) plus the hike to get home so we could attend midnight mass at our local, rural church, their first in the church's eighty-year history. At 9:30 p.m. we walk ten steep mountain minutes by starlight from our house to the church. A generator rented for the occasion basks the church in a holy glow.

Three hundred people of all ages are sublimely excited and immaculately dressed. Just before the service begins, Jean Louis (thankfully now primarily our friend and the church director, not our house contractor) asks Shelly to read one of the liturgical Scripture passages. We're the only foreigners in the congregation, and though we've attended the church for almost a year, we had never before participated in the service. She gratefully accepts and borrows the Bible to rehearse Genesis 22:1-18, about Abraham's faith, the near filicide of Isaac and God's provision of the ram. She returns the Bible to Jean Louis just before the service begins, at 10:00 p.m., as everyone clusters and holds candles outside on the church's front stairs. She whispers to me, "He said he might ask you to read, too, and it's in the old writing system."

About an hour into the service, as we progress through seven passages that recount God's salvation history on humanity's behalf, Shelly reads. She does well, though by now I am so sleepy that the service has melted into blurry surrealism. Some time later, the lector catches my eye and nods as he announces the next reading will be from Ezekiel 36:16-28, about God's anger and ultimate mercy toward Israel. I walk up. Adrenaline briefly makes everything clear and crisp, though I stumble slightly over the step up to the lectern. Ready to read, I look down at the strings of letters and words. Gibberish. The Creole I see, in the old orthography abandoned a decade ago, looks like this: "*Min, mouin vi-n gin pitié . . .*" The phonetic-based Creole I know would have looked like this: "*Men mwen vin gen pitye . . .*" Normally this would have been a surmountable difference, but now it drops exhaustion onto me like a thick, heavy shroud. I stumble and stutter and plow through the unfamiliar words—which I sometimes recognize as they come out of my mouth, sometimes don't. A third of the way through, I hear commotion, and a section of youth in the back left corner breaks out in suppressed laughter. Lucidity pierces my dreamy shroud. I think I just misspoke. I think I just accidentally said, "Then the prophet Ezekiel soiled himself." I pause, but the only choice is to plow back in, with two-thirds yet to go. Several sentences on, as the snickers continue to sneak their way up, I'm still uncertain what happened but mutter, "*Padon.*" "Pardon." I'm angry that God's vassals are so wordy. I conclude with: "*Sa se pawòl Granmèt la ki genyen tout pouvwa.*" "This is the word of the all-powerful Lord." The congregation responds: "*Mèsi, Bondye. Mèsi.*" "Thank you, God. Thank you." I sit, embarrassed, uncertain, tired.

But then—building, building—midnight arrives and the resurrection is announced. Everyone stands and starts singing: "*Viv Bondye nan syèl la. Sou tè a se pou pèp ou a viv ak kè pose. N ap fè lwanj pou ou. Se ou n ap adore. N ap fè konpliman pou ou.*" "Living God in heaven. It's for your people on earth to live in peace. It's you we adore. We're praising you." Again and again and again. Someone is ringing the church bell, over and over, keeps getting louder. Dancing and clapping is breaking out throughout the congregation. I've never been in the midst of such unrestrained singing, such surging joyfulness, continuing and bursting forth. An old, gray-haired, dapper man across from me is singing, swinging his hips—dignified swinging, bold singing, clapping, swaying side to side like an ancient jazz master. People keep singing the same song, somehow louder and louder even after ten, fifteen, twenty minutes. My wavering faith is buoyed by the rising tide of praise. Whether or not I had said Ezekiel soiled himself doesn't matter now: Christ has risen! The celebration continues, though not at the same fevered pitch, for two-and-a-half more hours. Then we all have bread and spiced tea outside before dispersing to our homes to sleep. I collapse into bed in peace. For tonight, all but a remnant of shame and doubt is washed away by the joy.

BUILDING A HOME (PART IV)

Build houses and settle down;
plant gardens and eat what they produce.

JEREMIAH 29:5

I'm sitting next to the exposed electrical wires, where there should be a breaker, near an unusable window the welder never returned to repair, not far from the unfinished cement back porch and exposed concrete blocks, under a roof that leaks in hard rains. Then there's the land I'm on.

The very first day of work on the house, we had tossed aside the remaining overgrown rocks from Lafrique's (the long dead uncle of Jean Louis) crumbled mountain house to build ours. Four hundred years ago slaves were first imported by the French from Africa (in French, *l'Afrique*) to replace the native Arawak population, who were quickly being killed off by disease and brutal forced labor. Then two hundred years ago the African slaves, many of whom organized after escaping up into the mountains, overthrew the French conquerors. Free, free at last—though still chained to the suffering of chronic poverty, foreign meddling and misgovernment amidst power struggles.

This was Lafrique's house, and we had built on it. This was Lafrique's house, and we had improved on it. What responsibility comes with getting a better house than the peasant farmer Lafrique had? We just wanted a simple place to live, close enough to commute, but not in the city. Still, nothing feels simple amidst too much history, suffering, scarcity. We started the project just more than a year ago and have now been in the house for about eight months. It would feel less visceral if we'd rented an apartment or house from a bourgeoisie landlord in a decent neighborhood, but it wouldn't really be different.

Several weeks ago on the daily, bumpy tap-tap ride from the office to our house, the passenger conversation turned to the occupying *blans*. I was glad the dozen people weren't inhibited by my (remarked upon) presence, though it's a little discomfiting to have those around you discuss—during your commute, no less—whether things would be better if your kind were somewhere else, far away, off the island. People were ambivalent about the American and then UN military presence, which had been in place about seven months (we'd been back for six months, after leaving during Aristide's ouster). As for people like me, most said, "Yes, they're great. They help us." A few said, "It's obvious we Haitians can't run our country, so we need them." But one man respectfully, firmly, said he hated to see *blans* in his country.

No offense, he said, but this place is for us to operate without their bumbling interference. A reasonable position based in fact. I was glad to hear his perspective and pride. It's an important question (for him already answered) both for Haitians to ask and for me to ask: Should I be here? It's not 100 percent good, us *blans* being here, but it doesn't seem 100 percent bad either. Is there a published guideline about this? A rule that if, say, 20 percent of the population wants you out, then you should go? Or does a simple 51 percent majority decide? What if only a handful want you there and would benefit from your presence—does that make it okay?

These join the other big questions that are easiest to push aside, like what do rich people owe poor people, what do global powers and ex-colonialists owe those whose ancestors were exploited? These are important questions, and yet what presses in each day is what do I owe my neighbors? Ideally I need their best efforts. And likewise, giving less than my full effort—that is, my Princeton life of only making small contributions, recycling and voting—seems to be complicit with and to handsomely benefit from sins of the past.

But I don't want building a house here to be a personal spiritual exercise (exorcise?) of cement and sand. Furthermore, do Haitians even care whether we live at a level similar to theirs? Would they rather I lived in a mansion, with a car and driver, an excellent mattress and a support staff, if that helped make our organization's work more effective? Our approach—trying to live simply and putting as much effort into the how as the what—has a danger of being too much about us, though we hope it is making us more insightful, better able to help and partner. And I think I can do some good here. I can't do 100 percent good with no negative side effects; I'm not sure life allows that. But if my being here is not for the best, then by all means boot me off your island . . . though this invitation is complicated by the fact that—as often happens in places like this—I'm the boss, the patron, the employer, the cash cow, the access to resources, or perceived as such even when it isn't true. Amidst so much poverty, whoever is bringing in money, or has that potential, wields power. How can I find a sincere answer? In that way, our situation doesn't resemble the prophet Jeremiah's at all. He bought land in his own land, where his commitment was permanent. Building a house as a foreigner on leased land, my commitment is more tenuous.

In a year or two, especially if we have a child, might this house and outdoor latrine with a concrete hole in the ground become an abandoned concrete monument to our flirtation with solidarity, with saving the world, with loving our neighbors? Someone else would be living here, but might our little haven then stand as a testimony to the incompatibility of my hope to be a saint with my expectations about family and marriage, with my innate American middle-class sensibilities and conflicted desires?

Maybe we'll leave. Probably we will eventually. Maybe one day we'll live in Haiti in a less simple, more American-family-friendly way. But now I look at international development workers or foreign missionaries who live here like middle-class Americans—with the appliances, SUVs, good English schools, TVs, generators, etc.—living drastically better than 90 percent of the people surrounding them, and it makes me queasy. Though what's the difference between living here like a middle-class American and living in America as a middle-class American, other than that the truth and injustice is starker when you do it here? Will my future, further-compromised self disgust me? Either way is worrying—that my future self might disappoint me, that it might not. Or is this whole experience strengthening me for future decisions?

Lafrique, what should my commitment be? What can I give? What should it mean for me to (okay, for people I paid to) have tossed aside your crumbled walls and built this home?

⌒

Daily life for most people in the country, including us, hasn't changed much from one leader to the next, Aristide to Latortue, from Marines to blue helmets. Well, maybe it's even harder to muster hope in what was already a bleak situation. People here don't have especially high expectations for their leaders and the international community, but even those (security from crime, affordable food, garbage collection) aren't met. One American development worker I know who has lived and worked in Haiti with admirable, even self-sacrificial, integrity for more than twenty-five years recently said, "I think Haiti has become ungovernable." I saw American soldiers perched behind sandbags on the consulate rooftop and French gendarmeries and Brazilian and Canadian soldiers making their rounds. Haiti is still a volatile place, full of seemingly insurmountable problems, some vicious criminals, and many more who are kind and also courageous out of necessity. It's unclear whether Jeremiah's prophecy for his own land—that someday prosperity would come—will ever be applicable to Haiti.

Yet I want to continue investing my life here because I love my neighbors. Before I came, this love was abstract and propelled by belief. Now it's connected to Grandmother and the four-year-old grandson and Frefre and Jean Louis and Maxime and many more—whom I care about and who care about me. Also it would be too devastating to give up hope that prosperity could come (in the full, deeper sense, not just the arrival of "democracy" or higher GNP numbers). It continues to be compelling to work with Haitian and American colleagues to help transform education in schools, community groups, organizations and churches. Of course this is a good idea, and it's so much more personal now that I know the kids who are going to school, have been to the churches that can be a life-giving community here, have been overwhelmed by the gratitude groups have because they're receiving training and materials they normally would never have access to.

The aim, including the ideas of Paulo Friere and others, is to provide people with helpful tools for determining where they want to take their own country/community/church/family, rather than deciding for them. Honestly, it feels absolutely quixotic some days. But if I don't have all the answers for myself or my country, of course I or we don't have the answers for Haiti. Better to work at giving people the educational tools to help find and make their own solutions, which will include how to work with outside help to create good jobs, increase local food supplies, tap potable water, plant more trees, slow erosion, boost security—the list could go on for page after depressing page.

Still, the small victories should be celebrated along the way, right? Like Wilio's own house now having a roof. Hopefully he will move in with his wife-to-be and little baby girl in the next year. He took us up to his fiancée's family home for a nice chicken meal, during which he confessed that for many months after his brother's murder he'd been scared to go down into the city. He brought us a few small plantain trees as a housewarming present. Almost every day we buy fresh vegetables from his mom down in the street market.

Our connection to the community is still complicated but keeps getting better—from the kids who call our names to say hi and ask us to bring them a soccer ball, to the people we sing next to in church and cram next to in the tap-tap, to the old women we greet each afternoon as they walk up from the market. Every morning and every afternoon we pause with Maxime at his Coca-Cola stand. He never fails to make us laugh and still complains about being hungry, but he also shares his meal with us or sends his wife over with a plate of fried chicken on a special Sunday afternoon. We occasionally lend him money to help with his Coke stand or his other work of making and selling charcoal.

Jean Louis still drops by every couple of days. We love him and his family—and also love not seeing him for four hours every single day before and after work. Our neighbor Edwa has been waiting a full year for Jean Louis to apologize for taking two of his trees, but we've kept up our part of the deal: when Edwa has been working in the field beside our house with his two sons, we've invited them to our porch several times for juice, peanuts, sandwiches. Sonson finished his building project down in the city with a different mason, but he doesn't give us rides anymore: he was carjacked at gunpoint and let out of the car in a dangerous slum, from which he then made his way to the police station, where they said the best they could do was give him ten gouds for a tap-tap ride home. Now we walk up the hill together.

Regular visits to Woshdlo are great. Grandma's embrace and teasing (mostly, "I'm going to whip you for not coming to see us more often") are always welcome. Meantime Grandfather, despite our pleading that it's not necessary because we'd rather not cause him a fatal tumble, goes off to scale a tree so we can drink fresh coconut milk. The friendships feel strong; the kids are like nieces and nephews. At least once per visit I go with David to get Frefre's cows from the field half an hour away and take them to the canal for water. It's been a long while since one has dragged me. I find out what David is thinking about school, the harvest, the latest dances and the latest village gossip. We don't need to visit Léogane anymore for Internet access, but sadly learned that the Internet café manager, Allan (a.k.a., DJ Action), died, apparently of cerebral malaria. We can't visit Nana or eat her coconut candy: one morning at 3:00 she got up, said goodbye to her one best friend then left for Guadeloupe. People often don't even trust family or closest friends with travel plans, so we didn't get to say goodbye. We hear she arrived safely. No word on whether she has found a job—that Holy Grail that requires dangerous adventures by so many Haitians.

In Mòn Zaboka many of the guys who worked on our house still drop by. Maxime, Wilio, Jean Louis and, well, all of them are still happy for an occasional sip of rum, which remains my main form of hospitality, though the consumption rate dropped significantly when the house project was finished. By the time we moved in, fifteen molasses-colored bottles of Barbancourt lay like happy shipwrecks in the garbage pit beside the house.

It's slightly disappointing, but I never heard the workers sing on our site. Perhaps we live too close to the city, where modernity has trumped tradition: they listened to battery-powered, static-drenched radios instead. I'm grateful first for their friendship and for their profound influence over my choices. Though they don't sing aloud about my stinginess or generosity, they still have a sort of lyrical power over me as my neighbors. This wasn't the case when I gave my money to the cashier at Wal-Mart or the local drugstore and then walked out with a product that was put together by who-knows-who in who-knows-where in what-kind-of-conditions on the other side of the globe. Globalization has important efficiency advantages but also helps us evade the discomfort of knowing the people we do commerce with (to our advantage). And it's not that personal connection necessarily precludes exploitation, but at least when it's personal the exploiter has more chance of understanding and changing—or at minimum might feel how much the exploiting costs his or her own soul.

We both *love* our simple little house, which (we can say in hindsight and with no more money to spend) is very well constructed. We even like the little castlelike curves on the top of the outhouse. The roof still leaks. We're enjoying each other the most we have since moving to Haiti; some tranquillity at home counterbalances the chaos and intensity of the city and work. The country is still unstable and in dire shape, but it's less intense than it had been. How can we not be grateful for glimpses of peace in and around us? Though we've learned enough to not expect it to last too long.

A YOUNG MAN FROM GONAÏVES

Speeding buses kept racing by without slowing down, with every cubic inch inside packed tight with people and chickens and sacks of produce, and often with a few more people hanging out the doorway as well as more freight and a crowd piled frightfully on top. The throng who wanted to go to Port-au-Prince was steadily growing, a battle brewing. After twenty minutes a large version of a tap-tap pulled up. As it slowed a few men swung up and on. Women holding baskets or bags of produce wielded them like battering rams to clear a way. Raw Darwinism on display, with the sole exception of a little girl about seven years old in a cute flower-print dress, who was ushered through.

Miss this chance and you might have to wait another hour. Everywhere you turn, demand is far greater than supply; you fight for whatever you want or need. Places on the bus at this hour were no exception. Somehow I snuck through with only a little nudging as people jammed onto the long benches that ran along either side of this old transport truck converted for passengers. Market ladies put their sacks and baskets under the benches. *"Lève pye ou."* "Lift your feet." *"Fon ti vanse."* "Move over a bit."

Tired after a punishing, hourlong motorboat ride across the Canal de Saint-Marc's waves from the island Lagonav, where colleagues and I had been leading educational seminars for a couple of days, I was thankful to find a narrow slice of hard bench squeezed between two middle-aged women for this trip back to the city. The middle aisle of the truck then filled with cargo and people standing and holding onto the metal bar that ran down the roof. Can't be shy. About sixty or seventy bodies squeezed in.

Several sharp raps with a baseball-sized rock on the truck's metal siding from the driver's partner standing on the back bumper was the signal to go. The truck jostled along. People started talking about life and the day in the market, then the topic turned to Gonaïves, which was not far up the road (about forty miles in the opposite direction). About two thousand people died in the flooding from Hurricane Jeanne a week ago (just months after another two thousand also died from hurricane-related flooding in a different part of the country). Mass graves were dug and filled. The outskirts of Haiti's fourth largest city remain submerged, with reports of people still stranded on rooftops waiting for the debris-filled water to recede or until they can clean their mud-filled homes. It was not completely surprising because ecological devastation, poverty, lack of competent governing, lack of a hurricane control center—ad nauseam—create conditions for mass tragedy. Aid has been slow to arrive because organizations can't figure out how to deal with the logistics, gangs and mobs of desperate people. Distribution has been difficult, dangerous, delayed.

Passengers expressed in various ways how terrible the situation was. Then a young man, about twenty years old, who was standing in the middle just in front of me, started talking.

"I'm from Gonaïves," he said. "Just got out."

Conversation in the front half of the bus stopped. He started telling his story. I had trouble catching all the details; his Creole was rapid-fire and a little disoriented as he jumped around telling of awful things, of the bodies, of water sweeping the living away to join the dead. Still little potable water, little food. Mad stampeding to get at any meager supplies that came in. Bridges were down; roads impassable. He must have slogged through muck and water to get out. His eyes darted to different people as he talked. People asked questions, expressed sympathy. He'd left his mom and siblings behind to find help, but he hoped to return soon.

"There's nothing, nothing," he kept saying as he stood, shifted, fidgeted back and forth. Then to illustrate his point he said, "These clothes, look I've been wearing them since last Saturday." That was eight days ago.

We all looked more closely, and he was filthy, a rarity because being well-presented in public is a high cultural value. Little bits of straw and other debris were embedded in his hair. His shirt was stained and ragged, as were his baggy jean shorts that reached down below his knees. He wore flimsy plastic flip-flops.

Then a middle-aged man sitting back behind him said, "Here. Take this." He reached into a plastic bag he was carrying and gave the young man a white polo shirt.

"Thank you," said the young man as he took it. The crowd immediately told him to take off his old shirt and put on the new one. When he did, a sharp, rancid smell released. Within thirty seconds, someone else down the bench gave him a white T-shirt. A pair of green shorts appeared for him. A comb. Someone else gave a bar of soap.

Two market ladies who were sitting down on the floor took to organizing things. They found two plastic bags. The dirty, smelly shirt went into one bag, which they immediately tied up. Then that bag and the other new clothes went into the other bag.

Meanwhile another seemingly poor market lady had taken a crumpled ten-goud bill (about twenty-five cents) out of the fold of her skirt and started squeezing her way from person to person in the bus and saying, "Just give what you can. Five gouds, ten gouds, fifty gouds, anything you can give to help him out." Almost everyone gave something. I gave fifty gouds. After almost two years here, it might have been the moment I felt most a part of the crowd: they did not expect more or less of me because I was a white foreigner, only that I share along with everyone else. After completing her circuit around the bus, she gave him a fistful of bills and coins that he stuffed into his pocket.

He was holding onto the roof rail with his right hand, revealing a few small holes in the armpit of his new shirt. He started looking around, up and down the bus. Then he started wiping tears from his eyes. "*Mwen pa konnen . . .*" "I don't know . . ."

"No! No!" People protested. "You didn't even ask for anything, we just want to give." "We're all Gonaïvians now." "If there were other ways we could give more, we would." A woman down on the floor just stuck a ten-goud bill into his hand. Jesus told a story of a poor widow putting two very small copper coins in the temple offering, all she had. A couple more coins came from another woman.

Soon after, our tap-tap broke down. Conversation turned to strategies for getting home and how long we should wait with this truck. From the sweating mass of bodies in the back, insults started being thrown the driver's way as he worked on the engine—attempts to provoke him into honestly revealing whether the truck was fixable.

After ten minutes we all got off and stood by the side of the road, but every truck and bus that went by was overflowing with bodies inside, outside, on top—unable to take even one more passenger. The sun was going down on this desolate landscape that was almost turning to desert because of all the deforestation and erosion, accomplices in the recent flooding. I slipped the young man five hundred gouds. Our truck started up after an hour, and we piled back in. A little slow, I didn't get a seat this time.

People were quieter now as we bounced toward Port-au-Prince. With darkness coming, talk turned to the general insecurity in the country. The man on the back bumper started banging his rock loudly on the metal siding every few minutes so the driver would stop to let someone disembark. People retreated into their own thoughts.

It's staggering how wave after wave of suffering, both individual and collective, keeps crashing down. Each person in the back of this truck must in some way battle, throw elbows, squeeze for what she or he needs. From a distance via the news, you wonder how anybody makes it. Up close you wonder too, but less so because you see the little things. You see the person beside you pass along ten gouds, a shirt, a bar of soap.

We finally reached our stop in the city, with the sun low in the sky. Everyone who was still on board, including the young man from Gonaïves, scuttled off on foot or to catch another tap-tap deeper into the city.

STATUES

These days I'm reminded of a man who once upon a time grew up in a place far, far away but not so different in culture, religion, constitution, citizenship or bone structure.

On his twenty-first birthday in this faraway land, he went, as was the tradition at this passage to adulthood, to register at the Coordinating Office, which required signing various papers and cards and smiling for several photos. They then pointed him down a long, smooth-tiled hallway. He walked and walked, paused several times to rest, sweating and thirsty. Every twenty paces a small, clean sign in twelve-point Times New Roman said Water Ahead. He would have turned around, but it was blurry back that way.

Finally he arrived at a door. He entered a room and stood alone, though it felt crowded with a million pairs of eyes watching and directing and waiting for him. He'd never been in such blaring silence. Two elongated basins sat in the middle of the room. They were painted cheery colors but looked like the top and bottom of a coffin. He walked to the middle. A small, cardboard sign with twelve-point Times New Roman told him what to do. He was twenty-one. He refused. He cursed. He paced. He kicked the wall. Eventually he resigned himself, figuring everyone else's birthday passed through here, and they all seemed fine afterward. He laid down on his back in the basin full of gunky plaster, like what they use to make a cast of your teeth before getting braces or a crown. Two faceless assistants came in and deftly lifted him out, leaving his impression in place. Then they helped him lay face down in the other half, which had a special breathing apparatus. When they lowered him in, he began to hyperventilate; it felt constricting, and the breathing tube was too small. But when he finally relaxed into the gunk, it actually became soothing after all the walking, after all the fluorescent lights. The faceless assistants pulled him out, and he sat in the corner as the plaster dried. He was covered in the gunk. He fell asleep in the corner.

When he awoke, he was washed and clean, sitting on a bus that was arriving at his home. There awaiting him in his own front yard was himself—cast in ceramic. He inspected it, amused, but it was also unsettling. Then in the middle of the night, he felt something was going horribly wrong. He found a two-by-four and ran out his front door and started smashing the ceramic statue with his face on it. The legs started cracking, and a mask fell off. He laughed because in the moonlight the face now looked like the face of the country's most famous sports star. A few neighbors watched with passive condescension. He stopped for a second, relieved, like he'd gotten to something. But no. He started smashing again, splinters driving into his hands. The statue's legs kept cracking, and then another mask fell off to reveal his nation's first president. Exhausted, with hands bloodied, he kept smashing through the faces of a top business mogul, a top religious leader, a top chef, a top model, a top designer and architect . . . and eventually the whole statue shattered into small pieces on the ground. He briefly felt free and had a sudden urge to listen for God's whisper, but he only had enough energy to carry himself to bed.

When he awoke at dawn, he quickly swung the front door open only to see that the Coordinating Office had delivered a replacement statue made from his mold. Night after night he smashed it, and the masks fell off, in different orders at different times. A few months after its first appearance, when he saw he couldn't permanently smash it, he arranged the burning down of the Coordinating Office. It was charred badly, but they didn't even bother rebuilding. The statue kept reappearing in his front lawn. Things were coordinated but not centralized. Then one day he simply went to bed early; when he left the house in the morning, he accepted its presence and kept going. Other times he took to dressing it up on his birthday or religious or national holidays, putting a wreath on it or some blinking lights. Once someone else tried to smash it, but rather than welcome the help and join in, he chased the guy with his two-by-four, ready to beat him for attacking it.

As he became a successful, well-respected leader in the community, the young men and women in their late teens would gather round to hear his stories and learn how he navigated into his respectful position. They'd sit under the statue, which he never mentioned, which he admired but also resented because he suspected he shared his success and power with the statue. As he got still older, he would finish his talk about doing things the right way to get where they want to go—and then wistfully, as though it were a throwaway suggestion, he would say there is this story you might find interesting in the ancient Scriptures, if you can find it, about three young men close to your age named Shadrach, Meshach and Abednego, and a statue. And he would remember his two-by-four, wonder if he gave up too easily, hope that a few of the women and men would find the story and, quickly wiping a tear from his eye so it wouldn't be noticed, even wonder if it still might be destroyed.

⌒

I'm suspicious of myself: I constantly cast myself as my own idol to worship, resent and serve. I'm suspicious of the politicians: they tell me and the rest of the world "You're either with us or against us" and try to bring us to our knees before national ideals to serve at all costs, even offer human sacrifices of our own eighteen-year-old boys and whole families of people in faraway lands. I'm suspicious of my culture: with its power over me, I'm unclear where I end and it begins as it guides me by ambitions and expectations into banks and malls and theaters to worship. I'm suspicious of religion: it too often simply confirms whatever the community is (whatever its theological or social bent) instead of leading us, full of awe, to humbly seek and then really act on, "If this is true, what does it mean for us?"

In my early twenties I was sometimes embarrassed about being American when I was out of the country, as I heard the envy and critiques. But I've become more comfortable with what the United States has right. Now that I'm here in Haiti, how can I not appreciate the silky concrete on a major highway or the high-tech machines and buckets of antibacterial used in a shiny hospital? Walk into a classroom in all but our very worst schools and try not to be moved to tears by the crayons, trained teachers, desks, lights, books and materials they have compared to the kids (the fortunate ones who get to attend) in most Haitian schools. Sip a cup of clean cold water delivered right through your kitchen tap. And though millions are inexcusably without health insurance, most can pick up a functioning phone and press 9-1-1, and people in a mobile hospital speed down the road and come to your home to do their best to save your life. In the contested 2000 presidential election, American power was transferred (albeit from one party of wealthy, powerful people to another) without a single shot fired.

But I've also become less patient with what's wrong—using our military for selfish reasons but not to stop genocide, hypocrisy on immigration, exploitation of trade agreements with weaker nations, the growing gap between wealthy and poor, lack of health care for poor children, the inability or unwillingness to see ourselves through the eyes of others, national complicity in politicians' lies, and on it goes.

I gave nothing (except my tiny tax contributions) to put in place what works wonderfully, and I don't know how to fix the problems. But I have decided how I want to think about the problems and opportunities as I do my little part. It's not original, but intimately sharing life with a Haitian family and neighbors has made more real to me how Jesus talked about family and how I want to think about being a citizen.

He said things like, "If anyone comes to me and does not hate his father and mother, his wife and children, his brothers and sisters—yes, even his own life—he cannot be my disciple" (Luke 14:26). He said, "There is no one who has left house or brothers or sisters or mother or father or children or fields, for my sake and for the sake of the good news, who will not receive a hundredfold now in this age . . . and in the age to come eternal life" (Mark 10:29-30 NRSV). Talking about throwing a lunch or dinner party, he said, "Do not invite your friends or your brothers or your relatives or rich neighbors, in case they may invite you in return, and you would be repaid. But when you give a banquet, invite the poor, the crippled, the lame, and the blind" (Luke 14:12-13 NRSV).

So as Jesus redefines family, I take it he's also making citizenship basically irrelevant and telling us we should hear statistics differently. Two billion people who are my family are hungry. How many in Africa have AIDS? Mosquito-borne diseases will kill how many cousins because they're poor? Every thirty-four seconds, well, something awful surely happens. The number of people who are homeless or clinically depressed or addicted to crystal meth? All of these numbers are important but also numbing.

The way Jesus tells it, though, closes any escape routes when he disallows defining the world as Us/Them or as American/Foreigner. My experience is that the Us/Them is real, with profound differences. Yet for me, shared life and Jesus reveal even more profound unity in which we're all transformed into Us, and all into Them. This doesn't allow the problems of others to be Theirs, which We will help with if and as We are able. The way Jesus tells it, the essential statistics end up reading something like this: I have a sister out there who is being whittled away, from life to death, by AIDS. I have a daughter who lives in a neighborhood where a random bullet might pierce her little body. I have a son who is without parents and is a two-mile walk from water that will keep him alive so diarrhea might kill him. I have a brother who was kidnapped as a thirteen-year-old and then forced to murder as part of a wandering army as he awaits being killed himself. I have a mother who never learned to read and never got to enjoy or share with the world all the talents she could have.

This redefined family—like realizing that I deserve nothing—is a needed antidote to my many forms of idol worship. I fail at it,

I retreat to my own country for safety, but repeatedly trying helps me pick up my two-by-four to beat/pray my idols to bits. And when they keep reappearing, then I'm reminded to put my faith in the One who ultimately turns dust to dust and makes life into glorious life. And I think the One who kept Shadrach and friends safe in the fire also wants us to take the two-by-four to our own idols. Isn't this what Jesus was telling the rich young man to do so he could be free to follow?

BUILDING A HOME (NEVER ENDS)

Shelly and I returned yesterday from a short trip to the United States. They're always a little upending, these trips. We've gone only a few times during the past two years, for organizational meetings and to see our families at Christmas. The sheer amount of wealth and waste is overwhelming; the first hot shower feels magnificent. We welcome chances to share stories of Haitian friends and colleagues and our work, and rightly or wrongly I bury the impulse to stand on a street corner (vainly) proclaiming Old Testament judgment and instead enjoy the few days we get to spend with friends, colleagues and family. Returning to Haiti after a couple of weeks feels like coming home, but at first everything also feels newly charged.

This morning Shelly left immediately for two days of work in a town near Woshdlo; she'll stay with our family there. After a day working in the city, I climb up the path alone, pour a bucket of cool rainwater from the Texaco drum over my body, and come inside to make some guacamole by adding lime and salt to avocados from our trees.

Suddenly, the sky darkens, and rain roars down. I'm jarred into absolute sonic, visual, emotional solitude. The canal that runs down the middle of our roof, catching the water off the tin, starts leaking immediately. My desk, where the guacamole sits half finished, starts crawling with a hundred winged termites and other little larvae I haven't seen before. Water blows in the back door and starts to soak the mattresses that we'd propped up on a chair to dry out during the day. All of this has happened in thirty seconds. Lightning starts hitting nearby. Rain roars. I light a kerosene lamp. As I move the mattresses, I drop one of them into the growing puddle inside the back door. I shut the door, then turn to see a twelve-inch-long, inch-wide centipede slink through the front door. Like the foreshadowing of evil in a bad movie. We get tarantulas in our house every few weeks, but this centipede is a first. Their bite is apparently vicious. Our cat can't help because the dogs chased little Mitsu away a few months ago and won't let him/her return anywhere near the house, despite our best rescue efforts. I take off a flip-flop and throw it down hard. The centipede starts writhing back and forth, convulsing like a demon is being cast out. I grab a broom, an ineffective weapon, and keep hitting. Then right behind me—*POP*. I jump, inhale sharply. What was that? Water had leaked from the roof into the light bulb, filled it up and burst it. Now a stream of water is pouring through the sole, bare light bulb in the middle of the room.

I finish off the centipede and sweep it out. Grab a pot to stick under the new leak. The thunder reverberates down my vertebrae. I need to calm down. It's only about 6 or 7 p.m. I want to bolt the metal doors and windows and escape into sleep, but I've tried that before only to wake up at 11 p.m. for a long, lonely night. Rain has lightened. I force myself to go outside and sit in my rocking chair on the covered porch. Face the fear directly, or something like that. Breathe each breath deeply, or something like that. Lightning flashes, freezing the trees and dark shadows into sharp photographic relief every couple of minutes.

The next night rain falls, but not as hard. Shelly doesn't return till tomorrow afternoon. Tonight doesn't turn dramatic. I go to sleep, and then the electricity comes; it's unpredictable but sometimes comes for a few hours at night. The light switch for the bedroom had been on, so I get up to turn it off. *Ahhh!* Shocked hard and thrown back several steps. I take my flip-flop (a handy weapon *and* tool) and throw it to turn off the switch. Lay back in bed wondering what just happened. Left arm tingling. Feel like a stranger in my bed. Are all the sockets around me buzzing, alive, ready to snap at my touch?

When I get up the next morning, my right calf is cramping. I try to stretch it out, but it keeps cramping badly. It's almost amusing. Can a shock taken through my left thumb and forefinger cause this? Jacob wrestled the angel, got a bad hip. I touch a light switch, get a tight calf and slight limp for the morning.

6

Next Steps

VULNERABLE

Framed pictures of smiling children are scattered along counters and across the office walls. The doctor asks why we're there. He's a brusque, charming man who looks the part of a Haitian bourgeois, with black hair and beard streaked boldly with gray. His office is in the nicer section of the city, sprinkled with a few boutiques and bakeries for the upper class. We tell him that a couple of days ago (the day before my thirty-second birthday) a "+" appeared in the little window of a home test. He sends Shelly to a lab downstairs. A technician draws a vial of blood. Five minutes later the technician hands her an envelope. We peek in on the way back up the stairs: "*Positif.*" The doctor looks at it and says, "Congratulations, you're pregnant. I want a sonogram. No horseback riding. No scuba diving. See you in a week."

The next day Shelly and I are on the back of a motorcycle taxi driven by Emmanuel on the way downtown, near the national palace, for the sonogram. We're directed into one of the exam rooms. Shelly slips into a thin, cotton, pastel green robe the same color as the walls. The doctor comes in and rubs jelly on Shelly's belly. An oblong shape appears on the screen, with, he points out, a little dot inside that is well placed in the uterus. He clicks a few buttons, drags a measuring line across the screen and says *li* (helpfully at this stage, Creole's third-person personal pronoun is gender neutral) is six weeks, five days old. The machine also lets us eavesdrop on the tiny, muffled heartbeat. For the first time since seeing the "+" our hearts flutter too.

After paying the receptionist twenty-five dollars, Shelly swings up onto the motorcycle and settles in behind Emmanuel. I get on behind her. As we wind through the busy streets, I feel a surge of panic. I feel more protective of her than ever before. In my mind I scream, "Stop the motorcycle! Where's the nearest Volvo dealer? We'll walk. Stop now!" (No, not one of us is wearing a helmet.) But it also feels wonderful, the wind rushing past. Our secret. Nobody else knows about this new, tiny life. My arms around Shelly, on her stomach, as we slice through the city chaos on the back of the bike. I feel like a fool for having her—them—exposed like this. Yet for a moment my arms feel almost strong enough to keep her and *li* safe.

This afternoon as we hike up the mountain, we laugh at how daunting this climb will soon become. Several months ago we would regularly come up beside Madam Sauveur slowly making her way up from regular prenatal visits at a city clinic. She's part of a large family we visit often and attend church with. They live fifteen minutes (or sixty, at her pace) farther up. During the last couple of months of pregnancy, her belly inflated like a gigantic beach ball. Some days we would come up beside her on our way home from work and join her as she shuffled along, little step by little step, one of her hands supporting her lower back and the other wiping the sweat dripping from her forehead down to her lively eyes and wide smile. After a few minutes, she would breathlessly tell us to continue on ahead. Don't wait for me. We would accelerate to normal pace. About fifty feet ahead, sitting on a tree stump or standing by the side of the road, would be her husband, a kind, thin man with a patchy beard. In his slow baritone voice he would gently drawl, "I feel bad, but I just can't walk slow enough."

∼

A week after seeing the sonogram blip, just after hiking home from work and beginning dinner, our cell phone rings. It is a friend named Wesley. He grew up in an orphanage and has been battered by an incredibly tough life, but he's a wily survivor. He's jittery on the phone: "I just came to the Baptist Mission hospital with my wife. She's pregnant and *l ap bay san.*" "She's bleeding."

He tries to explain. I'm unclear exactly what is wrong, but so is he. The doctors are looking at her. He has spent a lot of money, part of an advance he had just taken to go toward constructing a little home. He doesn't ask for anything. His wife seems okay. I tell him to call if he has any other problems.

An hour later, I answer the cell phone. He's more frantic still. "We left the hospital, and then on the tap-tap on the way home, she started bleeding again. Bleeding so much, all over the tap-tap." He took her to a private clinic. He didn't have any money, but they were treating her. It was unclear what was wrong, though the nurse told him they lost the baby. I head back down the mountain with a visiting American friend to the clinic—the same clinic where last year a pregnant woman had died of eclampsia out on the sidewalk. On the way, we pass Maxime putting away his Cokes for the night. He admonishes us for going down when it's almost dark.

I'm nervous remembering that Madam Sauveur recently told us about how she had gone into labor late at night, then started having seizures. Her family tied her down to the bed to keep her from hurting herself, then waited till dawn to take her to a clinic to deliver. She was fortunate, but the lifetime risk of maternal mortality for Haitian women is one in twenty-nine. (The lifetime risk of maternal mortality for an American woman is one in twenty-five hundred. The infant mortality rate in Haiti is seventy-four deaths per one thousand live births, compared to less than six deaths per one thousand in the United States.)

When we arrive, Wesley's wife, Shanta, had just finished a DNC procedure. He took me back to see her. The clinic is clean and orderly. She's lying on a bed with a sheer nightie on, no sheets, in a small room for two. An IV snakes down to her hand. Her belly is flat as a frying pan. She looks so tiny and weak. She's lost lots of blood, he said. The IV is for rehydrating.

After saying hi to her, saying I was so sorry, just standing there for a minute or two, I turn to talk logistics with Wesley. The clinic personnel are kind and professional but say they want immediate payment and that she must be out within an hour. Wesley says he doesn't have the money. We go out to the small lobby to talk with the cashier, pharmacist and nurse. I had fortunately just withdrawn money that afternoon, and my American friend and I could just cover the hundred dollars for the medical bill and medicines. Wesley is scared and wants her to stay here, not come home yet. What if something else goes wrong? I plead too. They say she has to go, and they need payment. Could we pay more for her to stay in a bed? There are no extra beds, and she needs to be out of this one soon. I call Jean Louis to ask who might help, and eventually arrange a ride to take her home. ("You're going to put her out, where she has to walk to the nearest tap-tap station, cram in back, transfer a couple of times, then walk home, at 9:00 p.m.?" But of course their job in the clinic is almost impossible too.) The nurse says we actually have to wait two hours till the IV is finished, and then she has to leave. Nobody likes driving around in Port-au-Prince at night these days; the ride won't wait that long.

We go back in to see how she is. On the other bed, a boy with an IV is shivering, rolling back and forth and saying, "Mama, mama." I ask Shanta how she is. She whispers, "I can't walk. I can't even move." As she whispers, I notice the blood stains under her fingernails. The sadness crashes in. I imagine her scared and bleeding on the tap-tap. I, of course, imagine Shelly and the new little life inside her. And in the midst of Shanta's sadness, the conversation swirling around her has to be about a lack of money and her imminent expulsion from the bed. This woman merits the best care all the money in the world can buy. What single person on earth deserves better care than her? By what right? During a pause in the planning, her husband leans over and asks, "Did you see the baby when they took it away?" She shakes her head no and then turns to stare at the wall.

A little later Wesley and I even laugh a little when we figure out the obvious: as long as we don't pay, they won't let her leave. The problem now is making sure she can rest tonight, though she won't have a bed. Wesley thinks he can find a foam mattress to put on the floor; the nurse and cashier reluctantly agree. I give Wesley the money for the next morning. We head out together—he to search for a mattress, my American friend and I to find a tap-tap.

༄

I want Shelly and our *pitit* ("little one" or "baby") to be in the best, safest, most experienced hands, surrounded by hundreds of thousands of dollars of emergency, only-need-it-once-in-a-million equipment, with money unlimited and a slew of Johns Hopkins doctors hovering in their white coats.

Give me thick walls, missile defense, mosquito nets, special force teams, Kevlar vests, high-yielding and strategically diversified mutual funds, job security and gravity protection fields around Shelly and this little life. Give me the Marines. Give me Jesus. Give me airbags and steel-reinforced side doors, a machine gun and everything else you've got.

But I want the little tin-roofed house too. I want to stay in Haiti, though it doesn't include these safeties, nor familiarities, nor family. I don't even know how to protect myself from ravaging intestinal amoebas. But I don't want to leave. I also don't know how (without a multigenerational family support system) we could realistically live like we are now with a child. But I don't want us sequestered from (or just occasionally tourists of) how brutal life is for so many people. We're doing some good work, but I still feel like I'm just at the beginning of living and contributing well here. Yet I also think I'm a better person here. It's been more than five years since that dinner with Vera in Albania, more than two years since we arrived to live with our Woshdlo family in Haiti. The victories are few, but I think I'm on the right team and in the right place, glad for where those beady-eyed fish have chased me. Deciding to spend some time in the United States might be as daunting as these past couple of years in Haiti, with some of the same challenges and some new ones: How do I live in the demanding grace found in and shown by Jesus? How do I live well there in the midst of an economy, structures and culture that have little concern for my neighbors here?

Here we aren't separated from our neighbors by the high walls that are standard for a lot of middle- and upper-class Haitians, for Haitian diaspora who come and go from the United States or Canada, and for foreigners who live here. We also live in a safe, rural area, which makes this more possible. There are parts of Port-au-Prince where hundreds of thousands of people are crowded in poverty and violence that takes them about as close to hell as anywhere on the planet, and we probably wouldn't last ten minutes, walls or no walls. It's important that when the local spring goes dry, or the pipe carrying water down from the mountain breaks, within two days we're out of water just like our neighbors—not bathing for a few days, conserving every drop, discussing potential solutions, contributing to the community fund for fixing it. It's important to us to be accessible so our friends and neighbors can drop by with stories, requests, concerns, a basket of plump tomatoes from the garden. It seems right to be vulnerable to and with them.

Also, vulnerability forces a kind of respect: if you're disrespectful, then it's possible, in the worst case, that someone might retaliate against you. It makes you incredibly mindful of how well you're living with your neighbors, how generous you are, how much of a disparity there is or isn't between you and them. Is there a home security system that allows a breach by an angry neighbor as a last resort to revolt against cruelty or injustice—yet is tighter than Fort Knox against a band of *Clockwork Orange*–like thugs, high on crack, armed with AK-47s, coming to rob and injure in their malevolent obliviousness? So is the ideal to be as vulnerable as possible to love and justice—while not being vulnerable to evil? Maybe this is stupid, useless bluster. I just want my loved ones and me to be safe. But I do need more than that too. In different ways, the urge to self-defense seems potentially as dangerous as, if not more so than, staying vulnerable.

At eight weeks the little embryo gets renamed a fetus. It's the size of a raspberry and taking noticeably human shape. Little arms and legs. Weblike hands and feet. Eyes are forming and wide open, with no lids yet to hide behind. Chorionic villi are the tiny hairlike extensions that hold the placenta to the wall of the uterus. A significant jolt could fatally tear out the villi, but those cells hold on tight for life. I don't know what all this will mean for what I believe, for my choices. My heart heard that little *thump-thump* via the sonogram machine a couple of weeks ago, and fluttered with cautious joy. Fifteen minutes later my arms were wrapped around Shelly and the baby on the back of a motorcycle, and my heart felt more vulnerable to being broken than ever before. These neighbors, this woman, this *pitit:* I'm scared, and I couldn't be more grateful.

⌒

We visit our Woshdlo family at least every month or two, and when we tell them Shelly is pregnant, they're thrilled. Grandmother keeps putting her arm around Shelly and saying, "*Mesi, Bondye. Mesi, Bondye. Pitit mwen pral fè yon pitit.*" "Thank you, God. Thank you, God. My child is going to have a child." All talk is about the baby. The kids work on potential names, gravitating toward a combination of Kent and Shelly that isn't especially fruitful: Kently, Kenly, Shelina, Shently.

As dusk floats in over the mango trees and corn stalks, the six-year-old catches me alone, makes sure no siblings or cousins are nearby, and says, "Kent, so when Shelly has the baby, will it be *blan* or Haitian [white or black]?" I smile and say I'm pretty sure it will be *blan*, like Shelly and me. He seems a little disappointed and is quiet for a while as we hold hands walking down the path to get water for bathing, till he says excitedly that Kently is his favorite name if it's a boy.

What is going to be born of the political mess here? Haiti is still swirling in a vicious political cycle that keeps repeating disastrously—with elections scheduled for later in the year, which doesn't seem to make people confident things will get any better. A few days ago one of our Haitian colleagues arrived at our office in his truck—newly bullet-riddled, including one hole at head level in the windshield between the driver's and passenger's seats. He, his wife and two teenage daughters had been in the car when police mistakenly opened fire. Our colleague hit the gas and saved his family.

The office conversations and radio chatter are uncanny echoes of last year's run-up to the February 29 departure/ouster/removal of Aristide—and of so much of the country's political history. Two other colleagues were just robbed at gunpoint when a man jumped in their car. I remember what yet another staff member told me during last year's political disintegration. She had voted in the first free election, in 1990, but felt nothing had come of it. "I'm never taking the risk to vote again," she told me, this woman who cooks and cleans and keeps things going at home and at our office. "It's not worth it. I have kids."

◦—

We hike down the mountain and ride the tap-tap to our four-month prenatal checkup. We're anxious because Shelly has had a high fever for the past twenty-four hours. I'm increasingly irritated as we wait for forty-five minutes. Finally we enter the doctor's office and sit in front of his desk. He leans his head into his hands and apologizes. Yesterday, he says, the private school his children attend was threatened over the radio by "one of the bad guys." The doctor is a school board member. Last night the UN promised troops to protect the school . . . then this morning they said they were undermanned and couldn't help.

He looks at the results of Shelly's lab tests and thinks a weak antibiotic will clear up her infection and take care of the fever. He then sends her to change behind a divider in his office. While she's changing, he and I slip into a too familiar conversation. He had received death and kidnapping threats because he works as a U.S. embassy doctor. Yesterday his doctor colleague who also works for the embassy was kidnapped. He gestures over his shoulder to the street where his hulking, embassy-provided, armor-plated, tinted-and-bullet-proof-windowed Ford Expedition is parked.

"I brought my son with me to work today," he says. "He's only in seventh grade, but if you say duck . . ." He smiles, shrugs. "This kind of stuff isn't new to him."

Five minutes later, he is moving a Doppler microphone around Shelly's middle. We haven't heard the heartbeat since the ultrasound more than two months ago, and we pray it's still there. He coughs and says that, uhm, it might be too early for this kind of monitor to pick it up. He keeps moving it around and says, "Well, we shouldn't be too alarmed if we don't find it." Then he finds it, faintly, then more clearly, the heartbeat. Thumping along. Thumping, thumping.

Shelly and I look at each other and, well, start giggling. Then he does too. Then we're all listening to this insistent little heartbeat, and all three of us are laughing hard.

How absurd and demanding, beautiful and fragile it is to be vulnerable to life.

DEPARTURES AND ARRIVALS

You can hold yourself back from the sufferings of the world, that is something you are free to do and it accords with your nature, but perhaps this very holding back is the one suffering you could avoid.

FRANZ KAFKA

The little sonogram blip grew. We continued working and bumping along in the back of pickup trucks and hiking the rocky path to our house. But Shelly wasn't gaining any weight and had too frequent fevers and a prolonged infection. At five months, our Haitian obstetrician ordered her home to the United States.

She started maternity leave when I reluctantly dropped her off at the Port-au-Prince airport. She traveled to stay with her parents in North Dakota. I stayed ten more weeks to prepare for the transition of being based in the United States. I worked from our mountainside home for five weeks and then showed up late one afternoon at our family's place in Woshdlo. They didn't even know I was coming for dinner. I stayed for five weeks, and when I left they complained, "So soon!"

～

This was my third time returning to live in the United States after a long stint away. My second transition (back from Kosovo) to be near Shelly wasn't smooth: her throwing a pillow at me, the Nachtwey photo book, the numb depression. But this transition has been the least jarring for two reasons. First, I was coming back to welcome my daughter into the world and was overwhelmed by the joy and responsibility of her arrival—and in some ways our little family has become the adventure and challenge I used to seek elsewhere. Second, I've been able to keep working with Haiti and traveling there every six to eight weeks. I didn't just leave Vera behind to take on unrelated duties. I'm engaged every day through my work.

We've moved to Florida to be close to Haiti. I've continued to support Haitian colleagues as they work to change their own country through education in schools and churches. A neighbor who didn't have his own home stays in our house on the mountain now, and I and other colleagues stay there when in Port-au-Prince. Most trips back, I stay a couple of nights with our family in Woshdlo.

～

The task now continues to be building a life in the United States using some of the figurative sand, rocks, concrete and not-so-figurative mistakes, stories and sweat that went into our Haitian home. All the generosity I've received will, I hope, continue to strengthen my convictions here in the United States. And so to make a difference I'm open . . .

Open to becoming much more radical and joining the revolution to overthrow what keeps the powerful with power and the powerless without. And also open to living and working against the system from within. Open to accusations that I'm not doing enough or that I need to change what I'm doing.

Open to pacifism and intervention. Open to giving and receiving anger. Open to giving and receiving forgiveness.

Open to ideals—to sacrificing for them and changing them. Open to compromise.

Open to engaging on issues anywhere on the planet and in my neighborhood. Open to finding I'm most helpful working here for the rest of my life, open to moving with our family back to Haiti or elsewhere.

Open to writing all this down and indulgently thinking someone might learn something from me. Open to putting down my pen or to picking it up more often. Open to criticism by whomever reads this book and then looks at my life.

Open to guilt. Open to grace.

Open to the overthrow of the government or to working with or against whichever one is in place. And open to the overthrow of my heart, because without that, governmental change isn't enough.

Open to God's guidance through Scripture, people and nature—and open to doubt.

Open to recycling and shopping locally and environmental carefulness and walking picket lines and supporting globalization and protesting it too. Open to boycotting Wal-Mart or shopping there someday if I can't afford what I need for my daughter elsewhere. Open to choosing a cause and giving the rest of my life to it. Open to the possibility that a lot of people who claim they know the answers actually do, though they probably don't.

Open to fighting with everything I and we have to try eradicating the diseases (medical, spiritual, economic, etc.) that we both propagate and need to heal—especially for the people who are suffering the worst symptoms.

Open to my neighbors in Florida while not forgetting my neighbors in Albania, Kosovo, India and Haiti, and open to neighbors in countries I've never been to and to refugees who don't have a country.

As deeply as all this has affected me, I immediately feel the gravitational pull to live a "normal" middle-class life back here in the United States. So I'm openly nervous because I'm sinful and do too many things halfway or get them flat-out wrong—and I find some parts of living in Haiti easier than living here. I want to keep making a difference—and to do it while limping beside Shelly, holding each other up. I want to be strong for my daughter.

I've never done anything so hard or so rewarding as trying to follow Jesus through the eye of the needle. Wherever and however this leads each of us, it's more meaningful, connected and true on the other side.

Epilogue, Acknowledgments and Reading Group Guide

EPILOGUE

ON MAKING A DIFFERENCE

This is a really personal story, but the book is also a kind of conversation between you and me (albeit pretty one-sided). On a plane, if a priest or pastor mentions what he does for a living, the small talk will likely veer into confessions about how the person next to him hasn't been attending church lately but plans to start going again soon. A doctor hears about someone's latest bodily malfunctions. When I've talked with other people about these things, one question has come up regularly.

After finding out what I do, people often tell me they feel bad about not doing more and ask, "I just watch the news and think, what could I possibly do to help?"

Faith, it seems, is following, not arriving. We each take the next step *from wherever we are right now.* Similarly, love is commitment, not perfection. Jesus was profoundly generous in inviting people to come along; a ragtag bunch have been around him ever since, which gives me hope. But he was also demanding to the rich young man and others.

Some people have to give it all up before squeezing through the needle's eye. But it seems that others start following and then, step by step, find the freedom to discard more of what isn't truly important. Either way, it's always time for the next step. Someone needs your help, and you need someone's help too.

So here are a few more pages for anyone who would ask, "What could I do?"

For everyone else, no need to go on. That's not necessarily your question, and in many ways my answers are already woven into the book. I'm grateful you came with me this far.

But for anyone wanting to get a little more concrete about that question, here are a few things I've learned that have helped me try to follow.

⌒

First, the answer to, "Can I make a difference?" is, "Of course you can." You make a difference in whether things get worse, stay the same or get better. Sure, at times the efforts will be complicated or go wrong. There will be frustrations and bad days. But you can help to make people's lives better.

The follow-up is, "How?"

No single answer to that, of course. Each of us finds our own way—within our circumstances, with our gifts and limits, following our passions, understanding the needs. The most important thing is to help, but this is life, not a formula. Follow where love takes you, engaging fully with your mind, heart and body. People need help across the world and also (likely) right in or near your neighborhood.

What follows is advice I've received and passed on. Normally I recoil from "Six Steps to . . ." or "Five Easy Ways to . . ." when they have to do with important things. These formulas are reductive, chase away the mystery while trying to sell something and set up the author/speaker as an expert on "how life works," which is a little ridiculous. That said, I've found these four recommendations helpful. They resonate with my own experience: when I've followed this advice, I've tended to do okay. When I haven't, I've sputtered along. The advice doesn't reduce the joy of discovery and doesn't over-promise. But if you want to start getting involved or want to delve deeper, these might help you along the way.

1. Confess and then turn away from what's blocking you. Jesus saw that the rich young man's wealth kept him from following: "Sell it all and give the money to the poor." Presumably it wasn't that the man couldn't have physically walked around after Jesus, watching him heal and hearing his parables, without doing this first. But the wealth kept him from being able to really follow with dedication. Jesus exposed his idol.

Identify *your* idols. What's keeping *you* from making a difference? Throughout this book I've named many of mine—from easy access to a bacon double cheeseburger to much more significant things. Since having a child, safety (both my daughter's and mine, so that I'm around for her) is on my mind all the time and calls me to worship and cherish it so that, like the rich man, it threatens my ability to follow with real dedication. What are you holding on to that keeps you from fitting through the eye of the needle? Next question: How can you give it away, kill it, disarm it, confess it, starve it, walk away from it? (Those are kind of violent images, maybe too male, but you get the point.) Repentance can lead you to freedom to follow what's more important, more rewarding, more helpful.

2. Start on a personal journey—along with some other people. "Journey" is a tired metaphor for life, but it fits this idea of following. Journeys aren't always easy, with energy surging and waning. Knowing this, get involved with a small group. Together you can learn more, avoid certain pitfalls, celebrate joys and find a way through the sadness (which will surely come) when the suffering of other people is overwhelming. The journey and the group will be different if you're a suburban mom, retired or in college. But whatever your situation, the chances of staying faithful to the journey increase a hundredfold (anecdotal number) if you are doing this with others.

Who can swim against the current of our culture and against the hungers of one's own heart alone? I have dedicated colleagues—

both Haitian and American—who are an incredible encouragement and inspiration to me, who ask hard questions, with whom there is sometimes friction, but all within a commitment to a common mission. This gives me strength. Other people can help you find both the right things to do—and then the courage to do them. Get a fuller view of how God's goodness is active. There is no easy substitute for the wisdom, encouragement and accountability of a small group of similarly committed people.

3. *Help people nearby.* The suffering and sadness can paralyze. The paralysis manifests itself in a lot of different ways: becoming numb or even more selfish or depressed, becoming reckless or running away. And so here's the antidote: Act! Move! Now! That the big picture is so overwhelming makes this really important.

I sometimes feel very discouraged about our work in Haiti because people face so much hardship and the change doesn't come anywhere near fast enough. So I ignore the big picture for a while. I focus on the people and communities I know. How are they making progress? I need to sit on the stoop and spend time with them, walk through the farm fields and ask questions. Look at the good things they're doing against the odds. And now living back in the United States, I need to find a soup kitchen or a community center or a library where I can teach kids or adults to read. Something and fast. Don't wait for the perfect cause or the perfect personal fit. Do thoughtful looking, but not for too long. Choosing where to get involved isn't a lifetime commitment. Meet people. Ask hard questions. Generate a momentum for serving. Stay curious. Don't get too satisfied; the goals are too important. Don't just stay behind the soup kitchen counter; go out and eat a bowl of soup with the people you're serving. You'll keep honing in on the most effective place to invest your time and resources: where it's hard and needed, but where you also find the strength to keep at it. Following Jesus—and helping other people—is active.

4. *Commit to a movement.* The last piece of advice is to get in-

volved with some kind of larger movement for justice. It could be for the environment, for higher minimum wages, for fair international trade policies, for a certain country or to end a certain war, any number of things. I'm naturally suspicious of movements, but this fourth piece recognizes that there are fundamental structural injustices bigger than any of us can change as individuals or small, local groups. The civil rights movement of the 1960s is a prime example. A personal journey to get over one's own racism or involvement in only local action to help a few wouldn't have been enough. Collective action challenged both culture and national legislation so that oppressive, built-in discrimination was changed for the better.

Yes, change happens. People, individually and together, can make an astonishing difference in the lives of others—in Haiti or in your neighborhood, for a group of people or for one person who really needs it. Each of us, no matter where we are, can start—whether with a simple, practical decision or with a radical change in direction. Jesus invites us on a fascinating, demanding journey. It's a wonder to see where it leads.

ACKNOWLEDGMENTS—WITH MUCH GRATITUDE

For friendship and inspiration: Craig and Esther, Jon Paul and Abby, Phil and Beth, Chris and Aimee, Owen, Brent, Luke, Brian and Audrey; friends, neighbors, acquaintances, colleagues and adopted family in Haiti for letting me share life with you. For partnership and friendship in work: Bart, Peggy and Tony Campolo, and everyone at EAPE; John, Merline, David, Jonathan, Jim, and everyone at Haiti Partners and Beyond Borders; the *Kominote Kretyen an Aksyon* and *Limyè Lavi* teams in Haiti; and so many people who have generously made possible the work I've been part of over the years. For writing encouragement: Doug Davidson, Brian McLaren, David Leavitt, Jo Ann Beard, Greg Paul, Tabitha Plueddemann and Barbara Chaapel. For my loving family: Mom, Dad, Jeannie, Steve, Chris, Vanessa, Julie, Darwin, Winston and Barb. For great partners in publishing: Dave Zimmerman and the Inter-Varsity Press team; and agent extraordinaire Kathy Helmers. And most of all: Shelly, Simone and Cormac.

I don't know the boy on the cover. I wish I did. To me, he stands there testing the truth of our love: there's no sneaking past his situation if we want to follow Jesus. To me, he stands there *as* Jesus: arms outstretched, inviting us down a path where ideas of success are challenged and where God is present in the suffering while wanting it to stop. To me, most importantly, he's simply that little boy. He's vulnerable, but there's dignity in his pose. His situation is grave indeed, with life on the edge and likely no education and not enough food. But he also might well be nimble with a soccer ball and quick with a smile. His parents would probably sacrifice to buy a fifty-cent Coke for you or me if we followed the path to their home. Simple but complex, demanding and meaningful, heavy but brimming with promise: that's Jesus' invitation through the eye of the needle, whether it leads around the world or around the corner from your house.

READING GROUP GUIDE

INTRODUCTION

Kent Annan's story is very personal, but it touches on faith, love, charity, guilt, responsibility and other issues in a way that is relevant to many people. For Annan, a mix of idealism and faith leads him to Haiti, where he finds an adventure-filled life and political upheaval. His idealism is challenged, and he moves through stages of guilt and discomfort—and then ultimately discovers more freedom in loving his neighbors and following Jesus. The following questions are designed to enhance your experience of *Following Jesus Through the Eye of the Needle*. We hope you'll enjoy this challenging and inspiring book.

QUESTIONS AND TOPICS FOR DISCUSSION

1. Who do you identify with in the opening story of Jesus and the rich young man? Who do you consider rich and poor as you go through your day? How does the way you think about wealth and poverty change during the book?

2. The author's uncomfortable experience with Vera in Albania (see the section "As You Leave the Village" in chapter three) stuck with him. His move to Haiti is motivated by both guilt and compassion. What typically motivates you more to help others: guilt or compassion? Is one better than the other?

3. Which parts of the author's story do you most identify with? When does he seem harder to relate to?

4. There's a striving, unsatisfied aspect to the author's struggle with the ideas of justice, as well as the specifics of his life in Haiti. There are also moments of grace—both in his experi-

ence with Haitians and in his relationship with God. Where do you see tension between "work" and "grace" in this story? (See in particular the sections "Seeing a Little More Clearly" and "Easter Vigil" in chapter five.) How does the author reconcile it? How would you?

5. The author's relationship with his wife—sometimes tender, sometimes tense—is a subject throughout the book. In what ways have your ideals had an impact on your significant relationships? How do you deal with these issues in relationships?

6. What issues does this book bring up for you about how development or missions work is approached? What are your own ideas about the best way to approach this kind of work in another country?

7. What comes to mind for you as an experience that has pushed you (or would push you) to your limits? While reading this book, were you motivated to do some kind of service—either locally or in another country?

8. The kind of service portrayed in this book is often idealized, but the author's account here is frank and even self-critical. Did you find his approach refreshing, disillusioning or something else? Explain.

9. Parts of this book are quite explicit about sexuality, fear and violence (for example, in the sections "Desire" and "Three Scenes of Fear and Improbable Vengeance"). Do you feel that people are open enough or too open about such difficult topics? Explain.

10. Some psychological studies show that a person's compassion peaks when it is focused on one person. With each added person (for example, now instead of one child, there are two or

three children who need school tuition), our compassion and the amount we'll give to help decreases. Do you find this psychological claim true for yourself? How is the issue of compassion and relationships with individuals brought out in the book?

11. Sometimes moving away to do something radical can be admirable, but it can also be an escape—from how hard it is to make a difference at home and how hard it is to become a different person. Is this okay, not okay or just something to be honest about?

12. When you look around, what's most evident: abundance, scarcity or just enough?

13. The author writes of feeling judged—at times by his own conscience, by God, by his neighbors. Do you ever feel judged by the author? Is it ever good to feel judged? How do you talk about the kind of topics in this book without making others feel guilty?

14. The author briefly touches on the biblical stories of Lazarus and the rich man ("Outside the Gates"); of the widow's mite ("A Young Man from Gonaïves"); of Shadrach, Meshach and Abednego ("Statues"). These Bible stories are found, respectively, in Luke 16:19-31, Luke 21:1-4 and Daniel 1–3. Read and discuss each of these stories. What does each have to do with the overall themes of this book? How does each relate to your own understanding of justice? compassion? faith?

ABOUT THE AUTHOR

Kent Annan is codirector of Haiti Partners. He began working in Haiti in 2003 after previously working for refugee ministries in western Europe, Albania and Kosovo. He is a graduate of Princeton Theological Seminary. Now living in Florida with his wife, Shelly, and their young daughter and son, Kent continues to travel regularly to Haiti for his ongoing work.

For more about Kent and this book:
www.KentAnnan.com

ABOUT THE WORK IN HAITI

Haiti Partners works to help Haitians change Haiti—believing that education is one of the best ways to do this. One in three children never get to attend school, and the vast majority of people live on less than two dollars a day. We make it possible for children to go to school and for their teachers to receive training to make their classrooms thrive. We also provide churches with engaging educational materials. One hundred percent of the author's proceeds from this book go directly to this education work in Haiti.

For more about this work or to get involved:
www.HaitiPartners.org

LIKEWISE. *Go and do.*

A man comes across an ancient enemy, beaten and left for dead. He lifts the wounded man onto the back of a donkey and takes him to an inn to tend to the man's recovery. Jesus tells this story and instructs those who are listening to "go and do likewise."

Likewise books explore a compassionate, active faith lived out in real time. When we're skeptical about the status quo, Likewise books challenge us to create culture responsibly. When we're confused about who we are and what we're supposed to be doing, Likewise books help us listen for God's voice. When we're discouraged by the troubled world we've inherited, Likewise books encourage us to hold onto hope.

In this life we will face challenges that demand our response. Likewise books face those challenges with us so we can act on faith.

likewisebooks.com